The Way of Jesus

The Way of Jesus

Re-Forming Spiritual Communities in a Post-Church Age

TOBY JONES

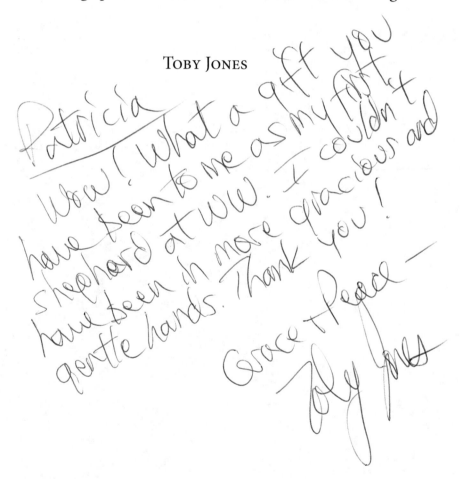

Patricia —
Wow! What a gift you have been to me as my first shepherd at WW. I couldn't have been in more gracious and gentle hands. Thank you!

Grace + Peace —
Toby Jones

RESOURCE *Publications* · Eugene, Oregon

THE WAY OF JESUS
Re-Forming Spiritual Communities in a Post-Church Age

Resource Publications
An Imprint of Wipf and Stock Publishers
199 W. 8th Ave., Suite 3
Eugene, OR 97401
www.wipfandstock.com

ISBN 13: 1-978-1-60899-152-5

Manufactured in the U.S.A.

I dedicate this book to Jesus and to the hundreds of inspiring people I met during this project who are endeavoring to live his Gospel in ways that challenge me to the core.

Contents

Foreword

SOMETHING IS HAPPENING. SOMETHING profound. Something significant. It scares some and inspires others. To the young among us, it is normal and almost mundane, but to the well traveled, it can seem exotic, strange, and unnerving.

Western civilization is in the midst of an *epochal transition*, a large-scale, societal transformation from one "epoch" to another.

An epoch can be understood as "a significant period in history," or "the beginning of a long period of history considered particularly significant."[1]

The transition we are currently in the midst of will change all systems, all standards, and all outcomes in society. I am not attempting to be hyperbolic here. I am, instead, being anthropologically technical. You see, massive, wholesale, cultural transitions are the norm in human history, and they are constant. The question is not *are we changing*, but *what kind of change are we experiencing?*

Large-scale societal change is always happening, in all areas of culture. We have seen it as long as civilization has been documented: human beings make significant changes in how they think, in how they use language, in what they value, in their aesthetic norms of what is desirable, fashionable, and good, and in the tools they use to support and create culture. The fact that change is a constant does not lessen the effect it has on us. Its regularity does not make it somehow less traumatic.

Let me briefly (and insufficiently, given the brevity of this forward) list the four epochal transitions in our culture of the last 150 years. For the sake of the point, one could think of these epochs holding cultural sway in 50-year blocks (a generation of people in length):

1850–1900	The Agrarian Epoch
1900–1950	The Industrial Epoch

1. Encarta® World English Dictionary © 1999

1950–2000   The Knowledge Epoch
2000–today   The Creative Epoch

Before commenting on these epochs and their relationship to Christianity and church-life, let me first make a few notes about epochal transitions. First, they exist simultaneously. There are no clean breaks between epochs. Rather, they layer atop one another. They coexist. But the differences are, nonetheless, meaningful on the grand scale as well as on a personal level. Second, an epochal transition is not a change that leaves the past era behind, but rather builds upon it. We move from one epoch to the next by building on what came previously. It is the success of the earlier ways that makes it possible to open the doors to new kinds of success. Third, each epoch rewards particular characteristics and qualities. Every era has plenty of enduring examples from the previous age, but the "social power" lies in the skill sets that are most current. The reward system of a society changes from period to period. In the Agricultural Age, one was rewarded for breadth of knowledge, fair tactics, and hard work. In the Industrial Age it was the ability to fit into a system and contribute to the whole that gave a person a sense of worth. The dawning of the Knowledge Age rewarded those who used the left hemisphere of their brains (the analytical, organizing abilities), while the current Creative Age rewards those who make connections, dream dreams, and find innovative ways to actualize them.

The move from the agrarian world of the 18th and 19th centuries to the Industrial Age was a dramatic one. The change from the Industrial Age to the Age of Knowledge has been even more profound and is still being felt by factory workers in the industrial belt of the US. The influences of these changing tides are felt in every area of society—work, home-life, city planning, education, and religion. The rise of the current Creative Epoch rewards those who break the rules, creating something rather than merely replicating previous patterns.

Religion is not immune to these epochal changes. Churches have followed suit and organized themselves according to the Epoch's cultural conditions. It is fairly easy to recognize a church built on the agrarian model—its building was laid out like an English farm and its leader was called a "pastor"—related to the words "pasture" and "shepherd." Often a church leader in the Agrarian Epoch would wear a stole as a sign of his role. It's no accident that the congregation during agrarian times was referred to as a "flock," indicating its need for a shepherd/pastor to feed and provide for them. The people in the agrarian church's immediate neighborhood were referred to as the "parish." Not only did all these props and titles grow out of an agrarian society, but often so did the congregation's intentions and programs. The fact that all these agrarian terms and trappings are still used in many churches today is evidence of the fact that our congregations have not successfully navigated the transitions from one epoch to the next.

The industrialized society also put its mark on the structures and activities of the church, but did so in very different ways. Churches of the Industrial Age focused on replicating rather than shepherding. Many of our modern denominations were created in the Industrial Epoch, structuring and governing themselves accordingly, with boards, committees, and officers. The primary focus of any given denomination in this industrial period became increasing production and distribution of its own religious "product"—mass producing more Catholics, more Methodists, more Episcopalians, etc. Each "company" sought to take over the market with its particular name brand. The rise of the urban city and the plethora of religious options changed the landscape from the agrarian society and made the marketing of one's brand of disciples more important that ever. It was also during the Industrial Age that many denominations built national and even international headquarters that were and still are reminiscent of the home offices of large, multi-national corporations. Individual church buildings during this period became increasingly large, branded, and domineering. Church leaders shifted their allegiance away from the "parish" or immediate neighborhood and toward those people who were loyal to their particular brand of religion.

The 1950s brought the dawning of the Knowledge Epoch. "Knowledge is power" became the call of churches, just as it did in the rest of society. In this epoch, the church leader became more of a *teacher*. Churches started adding education wings to their buildings. Camps were developed for teens. Sunday school expanded from being strictly a children's activity to becoming an important adult endeavor as well. Denominations created their own publishing companies for the purpose of developing and distributing their particular brand of curriculum. Sermon topics and titles were advertised on church marquees. The advent of the sermon as practical instruction was in full bloom. This was an age where what one knew mattered most.

It is important to remember that in all of these epochal transitions, those who had seen the greatest success in the previous age were at a distinct disadvantage in the newly emerging period. The skills that made one successful in an agrarian age were no longer valuable or effective in the industrial and knowledge based worlds. The ability to preserve the "party line" that served the industrial church so well was seen as a liability in the more open world of the education based model. In all of these changes and epochal transitions, the individual church leader and his/her local congregation were caught in a confusing and disorienting crossfire, rendering their tried and true systems ineffective, if not obsolete.

And so, here we are, in the midst another huge and comprehensive transition, as society moves from the Knowledge Epoch into the Creative Epoch. This period will be characterized as a time of making meaning, creating unprecedented connections, and developing entirely new networks, approaches, and tools. It is already clear that this period rewards entrepreneurship, art, beauty, and possibility. One cannot overstate what the emergence of this new epoch will mean for the church, its leadership, its mission, its structure, and its very life. The skill sets that will make a successful leader in this Creative Epoch are still in development. The kinds of communities that will thrive in a creative culture are only beginning to come into focus.

In this groundbreaking work, Toby Jones takes us on a journey into ten contemporary communities who are living vibrantly and effectively in the emerging epoch. He introduces us to the leaders of these creative communities and gives us a preview of what faithfulness will look like in this exciting and change-filled age.

As one of our pioneering and prophetic voices, Jones realizes that since we are at the front end of this Epoch of Creativity, there is more that we don't know than what we do. But Jones is keenly aware that this epochal change is upon us. It is real, it is definable, and it is the norm for many people born in the last 30 years. While this reality is scary for some, intriguing to others, and tiresome for those weary of all the change of the last 150 years, Toby is thrilled and invigorated by it.

In *The Way of Jesus: Re-Forming Spiritual Communities in a Post-Church Age*, Jones writes of what he knows deep in his being and of what was confirmed in the communities he visited—that this is an ideal time for Christianity to shine. Toby does not suggest he has the final word on what spiritual communities will look like in what he calls a "post-Church age," but he points the way for us, lighting the path by asking the right questions, outlining the key principles, and, perhaps most importantly, reminding us that the current wave of change is not something to fear but something to embrace.

Doug Pagitt

Acknowledgments

Randy Evans, for being such an encouraging, helpful, faithful, and affordable editor.

First Presbyterian Church of Harbor Springs, Michigan, for providing me the sabbatical I needed to bring this book into being.

Shane Claiborne, Chris Haw, Doug Pagitt, Nanette Sawyer, Cecil Williams, Janice Mirikitani, Liz Maxwell, and Tom Dickelman, for opening your communities and your hearts to me.

Dallas Willard, Brian McLaren, Doug Pagitt, Rob Bell, Tony Jones, Jonathan Wilson-Hartgrove, David Kinnaman, Gabe Lyons, and George Barna, for writing books that challenge and change people like me.

Janean Silvia Reed, David Richmond, Jess Rozga, Jake Deboni, Luke and Michelle Hillestadt, Ben Johnson, Kristi Murchie, Elaine Heath, and anyone else I interviewed during the research phase of this project, for inspiring me with your lives even more than with your words.

James Lin, for being the best host I've ever had and providing me with the full Glide experience.

My wife and children, for putting up with my crazy dreams and my writing schedule.

The Presbytery of Mackinac, for blessing me and letting me go to start Living Vision.

Julie Collie, for coordinating all my travel during the research phase of this project.

Liza Wilkes, for coming to New York with me and having a Wicked good time.

Tom Eggebeen, for your countless visits to my blog (http://faith4tomorrow.blogspot.com) and your deep understanding that there is no distinction between sacred and secular.

Wipf and Stock Publishers, for publishing this book.

Introduction

Signs of Resurrection

IN JANUARY OF 2006, I decided to attend a pastor's conference at a mega-church in Grandville, Michigan. The host congregation and its pastor were getting a lot of press, not only in my state, but throughout the country, and I happened to have some continuing education time saved up. With my MapQuest directions taped to the dashboard, I couldn't believe I'd have any difficulty finding Mars Hill Bible Church. "It's a ten thousand member mega-church! How hard can it be to find?" I thought. But when I got to where the directions told me Mars Hill should be, there were no signs anywhere. All I saw was a huge parking area and an abandoned looking shopping mall. I drove all the way around this run down super-structure, never seeing a single sign identifying it. Only upon entering did I find out that I was, in fact, in Mars Hill Bible Church.

I would soon learn that the lack of signage was purposeful; its leaders wanted to rely on word of mouth, person to person advertising. It dawned on me almost instantly that such an unorthodox decision would not only eliminate a hefty line-item in most church budgets, but, more importantly, the absence of any formal advertising would put the onus for getting the word out squarely on the shoulders of the community members themselves. I was beginning to like this place.

The conference I attended at Mars Hill cost $125 and lasted two full days. It was filled with inspiring teaching and seminars. But what moved me most happened just before the final session. Founding Pastor Rob Bell mounted the stage and told us that he wanted to take care of a little housekeeping. On the screen above him, Bell projected some figures: the total number of attendees, that number multiplied by the $125 fee as a "total income" figure, a lump sum "total costs" figure indicating what the conference had cost Mars Hill to put together and host, and a huge balance or profit line. While I don't recall the exact numbers, I do know that the profit line item was more than triple the expenses. Bell proceeded to announce that Mars Hill was going to give all of the profits from this conference to two micro lending agencies—one in an African village and the other in inner city Grand Rapids.

What impressed me about Bell's little moment of bookkeeping was that Mars Hill was under no obligation to tell any of the conference attendees what it was going to do with the profits from this conference, nor was there any need or expectation for Mars Hill to give the dollars away. This was a conscious choice that reflected Mars Hill's desire to do something Christlike with their money. The room, filled with pastors from all over the world, erupted in applause when Bell finished his announcement. We were thrilled to think that our conference fees would do such significant work locally and around the world to relieve poverty and suffering. Sadly, I couldn't think of any other church—including my own—that would handle its money this way. But it sure felt right. In fact, it felt like resurrection.

Less than two years later, I visited a Christian community on the other end of the size spectrum. It was a tiny, fledgling community on the near-west side of Cleveland, Ohio, which meets in its pastor's apartment. At last count, Pastor Meredith White-Zeager's Phoenix Project had twelve to fourteen people attending this homegrown, grassroots effort to engage twenty-something artistic types in the Gospel. The Phoenix Project hosts open mic nights in local coffee shops, sponsors poetry slams in community centers, and sees any avenue for creative self-expression as a place God's Spirit is likely to show up. The Phoenix Project folks may be few in number, but they are the very kind of people few other churches seem to know how to engage: socially conscious, artistic, multiply pierced twenty and thirty-year-olds.

The Phoenix Project community values individuals and their talents, no matter how untraditional they may be. Seeing one of their functions in action leaves one wondering if there are any other Christian communities anywhere that would even welcome, much less know what to do with, any of Pastor Meredith's flock. But being in the presence of this little gathering of seekers gave me a glimpse of what it must have been like to join Jesus at a first century table filled with sinners, tax collectors, and prostitutes. It felt refreshingly real and authentic. It felt like resurrection.

When an old friend in the Chicago area invited me to speak at his Christian community in Lake Forest, Illinois, I immediately pictured million-dollar homes, manicured lawns, and BMW's in every sixteen-year-old's carriage house garage. And, to be sure, Lake Forest and neighboring Lake Bluff have their share of traditional churches serving the rich and famous who reside there. But something very atypical is happening at The Community Church of Lake Forest/Lake Bluff. This community has its worship gatherings on the shore of Lake Michigan at the community beach from June through August. Then, from September through May, for a miniscule fee, they gather at the Lake Forest College Chapel, which has stood empty on Sunday mornings for more than a half century. The pastor of this community, the Rev. Dr. Tom Dickelman, keeps a very simple office in a tiny corner of a commercial storefront in downtown Lake Bluff.

This unusual church established a 501(c)(3) called KidsUganda, through which they have already delivered over 2.5 million dollars in direct aid to orphans in Uganda. In addition to these huge dollars, over thirty participants in this community of about 140 families have already been to Uganda, with more to follow, as three more trips are in the works.

In just ten years of existence, Dickelman and his flock at The Community Church of Lake Forest/Lake Bluff have brought Christ back to life, not only for folks in those two North Shore communities, but half way around the world in Uganda as well. What this little community has done has been as miraculous as a resurrection.

In my own community of Harbor Springs, Michigan, a couple of ambitious, civic-minded, home-schooling moms started something that may well be a part of this larger resurrection movement. They heard about a national organization called Mothers Acting Up—a group whose purpose is to help achieve the UN's millennial goals, most of which focus on eradicating extreme poverty and improving the lives of all the world's children. They then decided to start a local chapter here in Northern Michigan. Their first effort was to host a Mother's Day Tea in which they would introduce the millennium goals to the women who attended. They also planned to run an alternative holiday gift fair at our church when Advent rolled around. Their first gift fair effort brought a hundred shoppers to our church and raised $10,000 for local, national, and international non-profits, from a food pantry in Conway, Michigan to the Heifer Project. The following Mother's Day, the tea included a fund raising component, with an eye toward sponsoring a village bank in Haiti through FINCA. The goal was $5000 and the women reached it. For their next act, Alternative Gift Fair #2, the Northern Michigan M.A.U. cranked up the publicity and raised $42,500 from their 250 shoppers, and all that money went directly to selected non-profit service organizations, both local and worldwide.[2]

Two home schooling moms started all this, Kate Bassett and Copland Rudolph, both of Harbor Springs, Michigan. They consider themselves spiritual but not religious and have both had difficulties finding a spiritual community that they can get fully behind. But by steering clear of churches—and the committee meetings and politics that inevitably come with them—these two have reached people they never could have reached through traditional, denominational channels. They have also kept their overhead costs for each of these fund-raising projects to right around zero, upping the credibility of their efforts.

In the process of all this, Kate and Copland's Mothers Acting Up chapter has become a genuine community. They may not get together more than a few times a year, but they stay in touch via the internet, M.A.U. blogs, and the various non-profits so many of the women serve.

It just so happened that my church opened its doors to house Kate and Copland's efforts from the very beginning. Serving in that supportive capacity has been a privilege and has enabled us to see up close what these women have been able to accomplish. Their efforts have been nothing short of astonishing. Mothers Acting Up of Northern Michigan has brought together a broader spectrum of people than our church has ever seen and empowered that group to accomplish something none of them—or us—would have ever thought possible. It felt like a miracle, like a resurrection.

In the shadow of dead and dying churches all over America, I am thrilled to be discovering vibrant, creative, new, or renewed communities of faith springing up all over. Having learned from the well-documented

2. Kate Bassett, interview by author, tape recording, Harbor Springs, MI., 18, December, 2008.

failures of the institutional church, these alternative communities are fiercely committed to Jesus and his way. Given their genealogical association with the failed church, there's a refreshing humility in these resurrection communities, an awareness of just how easy it is to abandon the way of Jesus in favor of a lesser, self-serving way.

To replace or at least reinvigorate a Church on life-support, I believe that God is calling a very different kind of Christian community into being, one that may not even use the word "church" to describe itself, nor labor under the unbearable baggage that so often comes with such a loaded and misunderstood term. My research has led me to conclude that God is seeking out new wineskins into which to pour His new wine.

What follows in these pages is a coherent vision of what these new wineskins will look like. They will be supple, pliable wineskins that offer Christ's followers an alternative way to gather, grow, and serve in a pluralistic age. While some may experience this vision as "new," it is, in many ways, quite ancient. But it is, most definitely, a radical alternative to the status quo, "radical" in the sense of getting back to the Church's roots.

In addition to articulating and developing this vision one principle at a time, each chapter includes an up-close look at a particular community that is already living out one aspect of my vision in a compelling way. It is my hope that these community descriptions will help ground the vision in reality.

Constructing such a vision for times as challenging and change-filled as ours has not been easy. Finding or even founding communities willing to *live out* the vision I offer will be even more difficult. But what is the Church's alternative? Empirical research by The Barna Group shows that those outside the church have experienced those within it as hypocrites, too concerned about converting people, anti-homosexual, out of touch, too aligned with right wing politics, and, to top it all off, judgmental.[3] Are we simply to go on distorting the message of Jesus, or are we finally willing to try something that might actually help us better embody it?

The Christian tradition has resurrection and new life at its center. Jesus himself said, "Unless a seed falls into the ground and dies, it remains only a single seed. But if it dies, it produces many seeds."[4] As a resurrection people, we have reason to believe that even if what we know as the

3. Kinnaman and Lyons, *unchristian*, 27.
4. John 12:24 NIV.

institutional Church dies, a new sort of community will surely rise out of the ashes of the old.

What if a new kind of community with the resurrection power of its Lord is emerging to roll away the stone and lead Jesus out of the tomb? What if the new wine Jesus spoke of has already begun to flow in and out of hundreds of new or renewed spiritual communities that bear little resemblance to the churches in which so many of us grew up?

I've had the privilege of seeing some of these resurrection communities at work, living and serving in ways that line up with the actions, attitudes, and priorities of Jesus himself. It is now my honor and responsibility to share both their stories and the principles lying beneath them with you. But let me warn you: these stories and principles will challenge you to the very core and redefine what it means to be a part of a Christian community.

1

A New Approach to Theology

THEOLOGY MATTERS. THE WAY we think about who God is and what God is like is extremely important in influencing the way we live, the way we treat one another, and the way we interact with the rest of creation. As Emergent theologian Tony Jones puts it, "Good theology begets beautiful Christianity, and bad theology begets ugly Christianity."[1] There has been no shortage of ugly Christianity in America throughout the last several decades: Christianity that justifies racism; Christianity that allies itself with right wing politics; Christianity that leads some to bomb abortion clinics; Christianity that purposely and categorically excludes gay and lesbian people; Christianity that makes people feel good on Sunday without having any effect on the lives they live on Monday; Christianity that endorses material wealth and excess; and Christianity that condones pre-emptive and unjust war.

It is just such ugly Christianity that has led so many terrific, spiritually minded people—including many of my closest friends—to reject Jesus. This saddens me, because they are not rejecting Jesus at all, though they may think they are. What they are rejecting instead is the poor excuse for disciples that we in the Christian Church have been. As someone more articulate than I once put it, "Those who don't go to church generally don't go because of the people who do."

I've lost track of how many conversations I've had that begin something like this: "You Christians are so judgmental. You condemn homosexuals, women who have abortions, and even people of other religions. What makes you so superior to everyone else?" Would such charges ever be levied against the Jesus of the gospels? Or what about this one: "You Christians seem to think that the only thing you really have to do in this

---

1. Jones. *The New Christians: Dispatches from the Emergent Frontier*, 103.

life is accept Jesus as your Lord and Savior. That seems like a pretty watered down religion to me. At least other faiths ask you to actually live a good life." I want to scream, "So does Jesus! Jesus is totally concerned with the kind of lives we live here and now. But his life-altering message has been distorted and reduced to a mere belief system by those who have come after him. Please, don't blame Jesus for what's been said and done in his name!" Again, it is bad theology that has led to such a huge gap between the life and teachings of Jesus and the lives led by his followers.

Christianity has fallen so far from the Jesus it purports to serve. (For further evidence of Christianity's fall, read *unchristian* (2007) by Lyons and Kinnaman, who have done extensive research through the Barna Group showing exactly how deplorable the reputation of Christians is in the non-Christian world.) If there is any good news in all this bad news, it is that future communities of Christ followers are going to have to radically alter their approach to "doing" theology, to articulating it, and, most of all, to living it, so that it bears some resemblance to the One they call "Lord."

To shrink the enormous gap that the institutional church has created between the vital life Jesus exemplified and the far less costly one that institutional Christianity perpetuates, at least two seismic missteps will have to be corrected. First, we will have to address our long held misunderstanding of the word "believe," as it comes to us from the Greek word *pisteuw* (pronounced pi-stay-oo-oh). Secondly, once we properly understand *pisteuw,* we must put a much greater emphasis on right living instead of right belief.

Let's begin with a careful re-examination of this Greek word that gets translated into our English bibles as "believe." *Pisteuw* means infinitely more than any single English word could ever capture. In fact, *pisteuw* includes all of the following nuances:

> *to cling to,* like a cat sinking its claws into the bark of a tree, to hang on for dear life;
>
> *to pour one's self into,* like an artist or musician would pour herself into her work;
>
> *to put absolute trust in,* the way the smallest cheerleader has to trust the others in the squad to catch her after she gets thrown high into the air to do triple flips and twists.

Perhaps most importantly of all, pisteuw is an action verb rather than a state or static condition.

But we English speakers of the twentieth and twenty-first centuries have grown accustomed to using the word "believe" as if it were something we do only in our minds. To us, believing in something requires only that we give intellectual assent to it. For example, when we say we "believe in" ghosts, all we're saying is that in our heads we recognize the possibility that ghosts exist. Such an assertion costs us nothing; it demands nothing of our lives. We might say we "believe" a story our child tells us when she arrives home an hour past her curfew. In such an instance, "belief" in our child simply means that intellectually we accept the excuse she has given for being late. We use the word "believe" in a very simplified, narrow, risk-free way. Our definition of belief is cheap; it's watered down, and it has almost nothing to do with the Greek word *pisteuw*. And this gap between the Greek word of Jesus' day *pisteuw* and the English word "believe " in ours has created a HUGE problem, both within Christianity and outside it, a problem that simply must be addressed if Christians are ever going to remotely resemble the Jesus they claim to serve.

We can see the enormity of the problem when we examine one of the most important passages in the evangelical branch of our faith, Romans 10:9. Here the Apostle Paul declares, "If you confess with your lips and believe in your hearts that Jesus is Lord, you will be saved."[2] If belief here is simply a matter of the mind, then, according to Paul, all one needs to do to inherit salvation is accept as fact that Jesus really did come to Earth and did all that the Bible says he did. Salvation is pretty cheap with this understanding, is it not? But, on the other hand, if Paul is talking here about *pisteuw* belief, he's talking about something completely different, something that affects the way we live.

As one who has been involved in Christian churches for nearly a half century, I can state with relative certainty that only a tiny fraction of Christians are even aware of what *pisteuw* faith is, and fewer still actually live it. If I am correct, then millions upon millions of well-intentioned, self-proclaimed "Christians" have taken this single verse of Paul's and a few others like it, given their mental assent to them, and concluded that they are doing all they need to do as followers of Jesus Christ. Is it any wonder that those outside the Christian fold find little if any resemblance

---

2. Rom 10:9 NIV.

between Jesus and the one third of the planet's inhabitants who claim to follow him?

To better understand the life changing nature of *pisteuw* faith, we should also look at Matthew 14:22–29, where Jesus comes to the disciples walking on the water. The eleven disciples who remained in the boat, cowering in fear, exhibited belief faith, while Peter, who got out of the boat to walk on the water with Jesus, demonstrated *pisteuw* faith. In fact, Matthew seems to have written this story precisely to bring out Peter's unique grasp of *pisteuw* faith, the faith that none of the other disciples had. As the story unfolds, all the disciples see Jesus walking on the water. But it is only Peter who addresses Jesus, and what Peter says strikes the modern reader as highly unusual, perhaps even illogical. He says, "If it's you, Lord, tell me to come to you on the water."[3] Can you hear *pisteuw* belief at work here? If Peter were operating out of our cheapened English definition of belief, he might have said, "Lord, if it's really you, make the storm stop and the waves calm." Or "If it's really you, Lord, do a back flip with a half twist and land it without sinking." These kinds of requests would have reflected a "seeing is believing" mindset, for they would have put all the responsibility on Jesus to prove that he was actually walking on the water. Such requests would have been aimed at helping Peter give his intellectual assent to the fact that it really was Jesus walking on the water. But Peter's deep and unprecedented grasp of *pisteuw* faith led him to say, "If it's really you, Lord, tell me to come to you on the water." Do you see the huge and vital difference between cheap, "belief" oriented faith and genuine *pisteuw* faith?

The story is told of a tightrope walker who was performing in front of a large crowd. He did amazing things suspended a hundred feet above the ground. After his fourth or fifth trip across the rope, he bantered with his audience. "Do you believe I can cross this rope with a full-grown man on my shoulders?" The crowd encouraged him, screaming, "Yes! Yes! We believe!" The tightrope artist repeated, "Do you really believe I can make it across this rope one hundred feet above the ground with a grown man on my shoulders?" The crowd continued shouting, "Yes! Yes! We believe!" The tightrope walker then pointed to a particular man down in the crowd who was shouting, "Yes, Yes," and said, "You, sir, do you believe that I can cross this rope with a full-grown man upon my shoulders?" The man

---

3. Matt 14:28 NIV.

responded, "Yes! Yes! I believe!" The tightrope artist said, "Then climb up this ladder, sir, and join me, for I will carry you on my shoulders across this rope." The singled out man grew pale and panicked. He began backing away from his earlier enthusiastic "Yes!" To that man in the crowd there was a difference between "believing" the tightrope walker could carry someone across the tiny rope on his shoulders and actually volunteering to be the one carried across. But in Peter's mind and the mind out of which the Greek New Testament grew, there was no such difference. Peter's *pisteuw* belief meant that if Jesus were out walking on the water, then Peter would have to join him there as well.

The hard truth for today's Christians with our western mindset is that Jesus was never really interested in having people *believe* in him in the casual, intellectual way we tend to use the word. Jesus was, instead, interested in having people *follow* him and walk his path. Jesus was interested and still is interested in our being *disciples*, not believers, and there is a huge difference between the two. Being a Christian in Jesus' mind required and requires a way of life, which is why the earliest Christians were referred to as those following "the Way." Following Christ entails embracing and living the way Christ himself lived. When Jesus asked anyone to follow him, he asked him to "take up his cross and follow" him.[4] He meant for his disciples to follow him to the poorest places in town, to heal the sick, to care for the suffering, and to live in solidarity with the outsiders. Jesus didn't want people who merely believed in him; he wanted people who "*pisteuw'd*" in him, people who were interested in a whole new way of living.

By now it should be clear that the Christian misunderstanding of the nature of the faith Christ called us to must be corrected if we are ever going to lessen the gap between the way we live and the way Jesus lived. Outsiders to the faith have had good reason to dismiss our watered down faith as an illegitimate expression of biblical Christianity. But to make matters worse, we further widened the gap between New Testament pisteuw and our practice of it by making idols of the particular beliefs to which we have given our intellectual assent. In other words, having come to understand faith in Christ as mere belief, we then proceeded to make a list of the most important beliefs to which one *must* assent in order to be a Christian.

4. Matt 16:24 NIV.

So while Jesus made disciples—people endeavoring to live as he did—the Church has focused on increasing the number of believers—people willing to assent to the particular intellectual propositions that the Church has deemed most essential. While Jesus was all about right living—living according to his Father's will—the Church has been far more concerned with right belief. And once the tail of so-called right belief was allowed to wag the dog of Jesus' way, the institutional Church became arrogant, judgmental, and even malevolent.

Perhaps the best way for me to illustrate the damage that this second misstep has done and the immediate need for us to correct it is to examine the Church's well-publicized interaction with homosexuals. For almost forty years, churches across denominational lines have waged war and even split over this matter of principle—whether to include gays and lesbians in their congregations and whether to allow them to hold positions of leadership. We've debated this as if it were an "issue," somehow detached from real people, from children of God. Christians have lined up on both sides of this "issue," hurling Bible verses at each other as if they were spears. The national news has been filled with stories of defrocked bishops and censured pastors, leading outsiders to ask, "Why aren't you Christians this passionate about ending poverty and hunger, achieving the UN millennial goals, or doing any of the other people-loving things Jesus did?" We have been so passionate conveying our beliefs about homosexuality that we have failed to love homosexuals and their families in the process.

Several months ago, an extremely wealthy member of my church took me to task for making this very point in a sermon, saying, "But Toby, practicing homosexuals are living in unrepentant sin! We have to condemn that lifestyle and keep them out of our church!" I replied, "But you and I are living in unrepentant sin too." Stunned, he asked what I meant. I said, "You are going home from here in a few minutes to a six bedroom home valued at over two million dollars, a home that only you and your wife inhabit. In your garage are three or four cars, any two of which if sold could feed a developing nation for a year. I don't think you are going to sell that house or those cars and give the money to the poor any time soon. So, you see, we're unrepentant sinners too. It's just that our sins are different than the sins of those you call "practicing homosexuals.""

Lost in all our passionate, "Christian" debate about homosexuality have been the people behind the "issue," not only the real men, women, and children who are trying to make sense of their sexual orientations, but their families. Lost also has been Jesus and his well-documented inclusion of all people—sinners, tax collectors, prostitutes, and more.

So where has Jesus been amidst all of our principled blather? At some point, any genuine disciple of the Nazarene must ask, "What would Jesus do with a gay, lesbian, bisexual, or transgender person who sought fellowship and involvement in his way?" He welcomed Mary Magdelene. He accepted and later built his church on Peter. He broke bread with Judas. He went to stay in the home of Zacchaeus, a corrupt tax collector. He received the sacrament of anointing from a prostitute and called it "beautiful." His longest conversation on record was with a Samaritan woman who had had five husbands and was living with a sixth. And perhaps the most illustrative example of Jesus' radical inclusiveness comes in his interaction with the woman caught in adultery in John 8:2–11. For the Pharisees, who apprehended this woman, there was an important principle and belief at stake: adultery is wrong and must be punished. For Jesus, a life was at stake. One of his Father's own children was right in front of him, caught in the act, about to be stoned to death. Jesus' point in protecting this woman was neither to excuse nor condone adultery. His point was to show the Pharisees and those who would come after them that we cannot love God without loving and protecting his precious children. For Jesus, it was always people before principles, mercy not sacrifice, forgiveness rather than judgment. The job of the Christ follower, as best we can tell from both Jesus' actions and teachings in John, chapter 8, is to be forgiving and merciful, but, even more than that, to avoid judging and condemning others.

But with homosexuals, the Church has wanted to argue about principles and protect the "purity" of our church. This is what happens when a church decides that right belief is more important than Christlike living. Once we Christians arrive at what we think the right belief is in some particular situation—that homosexuality is wrong and must be condemned—then even the very actions and teachings of Jesus himself are not enough to change our minds, much less our hearts or our behavior. When we exalt belief over behavior and dogma over discipleship, we come to think that being a Christian means saying yes to a list of theological doctrines like the resurrection, the virgin birth, the second coming, or the inerrancy of scripture. Being a Christian means nothing of the sort when we take into account the original Greek and what Jesus and Paul meant when they used the word *pisteuw*. Being a Christian in Jesus' mind meant being a disciple, and being a disciple has everything to do with how we live and how we treat one another.

This is why I am convinced that Christian communities in the future will approach the theological enterprise in a completely different, much more humble way. They will begin by recognizing that all theology is "a calculated verbal idolatry," as a friend's former professor once put it. Any time we try to speak of God, we run the risk of creating another golden calf, an idol, a man-made representation of God in words. And even our very best verbal attempts to say something—anything—about God are imperfect and to some extent untrue the moment the words come out of our mouths. As Emergent scholar and spokesperson Tony Jones has said, "Theology is temporary . . . To assume that our convictions about God are somehow timeless is the deepest arrogance, and it establishes an imperialistic attitude that has a chilling effect on the honest conversation that's needed for theology to progress." [5] Barbara Brown Taylor articulated this same danger in her recent work, *An Altar in the World*. "No matter how hard I try to say something true about God, the reality of God will eclipse my best words."[6] While this doesn't mean we should stop trying to articulate who we think God is and what we believe about God, it does mean we should be extremely humble and reticent about constructing hard and fast doctrines or dogmas. Contemporary theologian and mega-church pastor Rob Bell sees the theological enterprise like painting a work of art. No single work of art brings about the necessity for other artists to cease the artistic enterprise. Likewise, the art of theology is ongoing, never ending, and all of us, Bell believes, are encouraged to pick up a brush.[7]

I saw the very approach to theology I'm advocating at a wonderful spiritual community in the Wicker Park neighborhood of Chicago, Wicker Park Grace (WPG). This fledgling community of thirty-five to forty participants (they don't call themselves members for reasons which should become obvious) meets for sacred meals, theology pubs, book groups, art projects, and fellowship. During a sacred meal and celebration of the Lord's Supper in mid-April of 2009, Pastor Nanette Sawyer began the

5. Jones, *Dispatches from the Emergent Frontier*, 114.

6. Brown Taylor, *An Altar in the World: A Geography of Faith*, 7.

7. Bell, *Velvet Elvis: Repainting the Christian Faith*, 010–014.

gathering by reminding the group of the recently celebrated events of Holy Week, using them to set the context for the evening's theme: atonement. She outlined the various atonement theories that have emerged through the centuries, as Christians struggled to make sense of the cross and its meaning for them. She gave everyone a handout with the five most famous atonement theories. Each was presented in a very open, respectful way, noting the century in which each theory seems to have emerged and the person or persons most responsible for espousing each interpretation. She accomplished this in a few minutes. She then shared a personal story regarding the particular atonement theory she had been brought up with in her church.

"I was about 10 and I remember my pastor telling me that 'Jesus died to pay for my sins' and that I 'needed to believe that to be a Christian.' I told him that 'I must not be a Christian' and stopped going to church."[8] Sawyer's openness about her own struggles with atonement gave us all the freedom to enter the ensuing discussion with no pressure to agree, conform, or even arrive at an answer. Her introductory remarks ended with an invitation for us all to participate in this ongoing theological process, "adding our voices to the dynamic conversation engaging this mystery."[9] We broke into small groups, where we each shared the atonement theory we had grown up with, along with the one that made the most sense to us currently. We were also invited to share whatever questions we still had.

The discussion in my group was wonderfully vibrant and genuinely open. Here are just a few of the remarks I recorded:

> *I grew up with the four spiritual laws and that whole emphasis on our depravity.*

> *I was hammered with the notion that someone had to pay for my wickedness. That was the purpose of the cross, I guess. It never really worked for me because I just don't see us as so evil. Where's the grace in that?*

> *The problem I have with all these (atonement theories) is that they focus so much on Jesus' death that they wind up trivializing his life. They also trivialize the resurrection by reducing it to some magic trick instead of the end result of a life lived for God, to better the world.*

> *I think before we can buy into any of these theories we need to ask what sin is. If sin is breaking some law of God, then I guess a legal, punitive understanding of the cross like the Penal Substitution theory makes the*

8. Nanette Sawyer, Sacred Meal, Wicker Park Grace, Chicago, April 19, 2009.

9. Ibid.

most sense. But if my sin is brokenness or addiction, then it seems the Eastern Orthodox notion of Theosis or the Subjective Transformation theories are more helpful.[10]

For me, the discussion was on or even above the level of those I had at Princeton Seminary during my M.Div training. But the beauty of the discussion at Wicker Park Grace is that it didn't end in some move toward uniformity or agreement. The whole group sensed that this was a conversation that had no end and no definitive answer. Thanks to Nanette's leadership and genuinely open approach, we all had been treated to a helpful introduction to the five most influential atonement theories, along with the invitation to develop our own thinking about them as well.

The gathering then moved to a celebration of the Lord's Supper. Our participation in that sacred ritual was made particularly powerful by the fact that we were all equally welcome at this table, regardless of which atonement theory we liked the best. For throughout our evening together, Nanette had successfully conveyed the deep truth that we are not united by our theologies or particular beliefs. For all beliefs are human articulations, "calculated verbal idolatries." We are instead united by God's abundant, free-flowing grace, and our sharing of the bread and cup affirmed that beyond-words truth.

That poignant spiritual reality was made even more profound by the music that accompanied the Lord's Supper and guided us through the liturgy. Wicker Park Grace's musicians compose much of the music and lyrics used in all their gatherings. The night I joined their sacred meal, Rob Clearfield—WPG music director—unveiled his recently completed original communion liturgy, which was thoughtful and beautifully coherent. His jazz background was evident in the unique chord progressions, while his lyrics were a wonderful reflection of WPG's seekers' approach to theology. When I mentioned to Nanette just how moving the simple, Taize-like communion liturgy was, she said, "We emphasize around here that liturgy originally meant "work of the people." So having musicians actively and effectively doing that work within and as a part of our community is amazing."[11] For me it further emphasized the integrity of Wicker Park Grace—integrity in the sense of all its parts fitting and functioning together in a coherent whole.

10. Participants, Sacred Meal, Wicker Park Grace, Chicago, April 19, 2009.

11. Nanette Sawyer, interview by author, tape recording, Wicker Park, IL., April 20, 2009.

After the service, I was able to converse with several members of the Wicker Park Grace community, as we seamlessly moved from one table to another. One twenty-five-year-old grad student noted that, "Jesus had no intention of establishing a religion or a theological system, particularly one that would give people license to judge and exclude others. Theological differences and varying interpretations of doctrines are all fine here. That's a big part of why I'm at Wicker Park Grace."[12]

I offered that in today's ever-shrinking global society, any faith that uses its belief system to categorically condemn those who believe differently is not likely to survive, much less thrive in the years to come. The literature and web info of WPG puts it this way: "At Wicker Park Grace, we are more concerned about our center rather than our boundaries . . . We see ourselves as participants in the dynamic conversation that has been Christianity for centuries. We ask questions; we respect differences of ideas."[13] Nanette later emphasized that "there is a center toward which we are all moving, but there are no lines or boundaries around us."[14]

When it comes to the kinds of theological lines in the sand for which we Christians have become so famous, Pastor Sawyer has a refreshing approach. "Around what are we drawing lines and boundaries?" she asks. "Is the line between membership and non-membership? Every idea is just that—an idea. I have deep, intense convictions and ideas about God and faith that I am unlikely to let go of. But I won't draw some line around the faith based on them or draw a line between me and another person because of them. I will continue to express my convictions as I also seek to understand people's different ideas." She continued, "At WPG we don't think of ourselves as having some doctrinal line which one must step over to be a part of us. There is not some fence around our community or some gate one must go through. There is, instead, a center that people go toward, away from, and around. For us, it is our relationships with one another that hold us together."[15]

Not one to accept the pastor's assessment of her own community at face value, I made a point of setting up several interviews with other Wicker Park Grace folks. I had dinner with Jake Deboni and Jesse Rozga

12. Participant, Sacred Meal, Wicker Park Grace, Chicago, April 19, 2009.

13. www.wickerparkgrace.net.

14. Sawyer, interview.

15. Ibid.

at a place called "Noodles," which is on Damen, right off the blue line. They'd been participating in Wicker Park Grace for about eight months when we spoke. Jesse is the Director of the Glen Elyn Children's Resource Center, providing literacy and life skills to low income children. Jake has been using his linguistics degree to teach ESL, but is about to start nursing school at Loyola. His dream is to provide basic health care in remote rural communities where there is no other access.

> Jesse: *My experience with Mission Year with Bart Campolo really changed me and my approach to faith. That was a year of intense service with the poor in Chicago. I lived extremely simply and loved it. Then, right after we got married, we went to India for a couple months, volunteering in a TB clinic, then to Morocco and Thailand. Coming back to the States wasn't easy. We tried several churches, ones that probably would have worked for us before that trip. But our values had changed. Our lifestyle was transformed by the whole overseas experience and exposure to real poverty.*

> Jake: *At most churches, the whole way people interact is to go straight from church to some restaurant where they spend forty bucks on brunch and talk about stuff that doesn't have anything to do with their faith. That was really hard for us and made us feel even more alienated from these communities we were trying to become a part of.*

> Jesse: *Yeah. I was always feeling weird and out of place in churches. Once we found Wicker Park Grace, we never looked back. It's a place where we are free to be who we are, to be real with others who are truly willing to have open dialogue. In fact, if there's one thing that keeps me plugged into Wicker Park Grace, it's that I can speak honestly with others about touchy subjects, disagree with them, and still not feel bad. There are no assumptions so there is no shame. Our loving relationships with each other always take precedence over our opinions and interpretations. For instance, there's this guy in our community who is gay. He has a committed partner, and a while back they were talking at WPG about having some reconciliation event for gays and lesbians who had been ostracized from churches. I'm not particularly drawn to the gay lifestyle, nor am I an advocate for gay causes. But Rick has become a good friend of mine. So I went to the reconciliation service to support him and to honor our friendship. He knows how I feel and where I'm coming from. It meant a lot to him that I was there, and I'm really glad I went. I learned a lot and thought the whole thing was really beautiful.*

Jake: *Yeah. And experiences like Jess is talking about speak to how scripture is treated at Wicker Park Grace. It's never called upon to refute someone's experience or lifestyle. It's more like we read it together and talk about the possibilities, various interpretations, and what the implications of each might be. I had really grown to hate all the proof-based theology I'd come to expect from most Christians, where everyone uses this passage or that passage to prove their point. During grad school, when I took my first trip to India—alone for 2 months— I came to understand that nobody really knows what they're talking about when it comes to God and ultimate Truth. Everyone's view at some point is based on certain un-provable assumptions and suppositions. So shouldn't we all be a lot more humble in asserting our beliefs and opinions? In this community (WPG) I've been able to see and hear diverging thoughts and interpretations that are equally beautiful and not at all fear based.*

Jesse: *I grew up in a family that read scripture together every single day — family devotions. I came to "know" a lot of scripture, but I also got so guilted into reading it, that eventually I started feeling my relationship with God was completely contingent on whether or not I did my daily devotions. Then I started reading a lot of Mother Teresa, and I started to realize that doing what scripture says is perhaps the most important thing, loving others as Christ loved us. There are a lot of people who know a lot of scripture but never get around to doing it.*

Jake: *WPG has helped me recognize that there are other understandings of Christianity and scripture than those I grew up with. It's been great to get away from fear-based, 'there's only one way' theology and into something much more positive, open, and beautiful.*

Jesse: *I'm grateful to Wicker Park Grace for helping me feel less crazy and alone in how I understand and practice the Christian faith. I've gained a new sense of freedom and found support for our ongoing effort to align our lives with the life of Christ.*[16]

One finds a refreshing humility in Pastor Sawyer and in her community. This commitment to putting their relationships with one another above doctrine is genuinely Christlike and bears a much more authentic witness to him than a million doctrinal lines in the sand. William J. Carl III, President of Pittsburgh Theological Seminary, puts it this way: "Real

16. Jake Deboni and Jesse Rozga, interview by author, tape recording, Chicago, IL., 21 April 2009.

friendship in Christ means that we have the right to disagree knowing that mutual affection and respect are not at stake."[17] It is precisely this subjugating of doctrine and biblical interpretations that will characterize effective, thriving Christian communities in the future.

We know that communities like Wicker Park Grace are the future by virtue of the age of their participants. Most WPG'ers are in their mid-twenties. Their leader, at forty-eight, is the second oldest participant in the entire community. Compare their average age—about twenty-six at Wicker Park Grace—to that of the larger Church. In my denomination, the average age is nearing sixty, and Presbyterians are constantly asking, "Where are all the young people? Why don't any young people come to church anymore?" The answer is that young people are finding communities where there are centers instead of lines, bridges instead of fences, relationships instead of boundaries, and humility instead of arrogance. Karl Barth was right when he noted that, "As ministers we ought to speak of God. We are humans, however, and so cannot speak of God. We ought, therefore, to recognize both our obligation and our inability and by that very recognition give God the glory."[18]

Comedian Dennis Miller was famous for his hard-hitting rants on topics ranging from the houses of Congress to the lifestyles of Hollywood divas. His iconoclastic diatribes, no matter how embittered and filled with evidence for his viewpoint, always ended with his signature tag line, "Of course, that's just my opinion. I could be wrong." I've often wondered what would happen if we preachers ended our weekly sermons that way. Better still, what if our denominations ended their various position papers and doctrinal rulings that way? Do we have the humility within us to do so? Do we have the appropriate reverence and awe of what Rudolf Otto called "the Mysterium Tremendum" to see to it that even our words and ideas bow before Him?

Wicker Park Grace's approach to theology and belief provides us with a wonderful model for the future. They have embraced the tremendous diversity within American society without fear. They hunger for interfaith and inter-religious dialogue, for they see the Christian conversation as ongoing, unfinished, and filled with infinite possibilities for their own participation. They have a leader who lays out the many ways to under-

17. William J. Carl, "Preaching in a church where the culture needs to change," in Carl, William J. *Best Advice* (Louisville: Westminster John Knox Press, 2009), 40.

18. James C. Howell, "Don't Take My Advice," in Carl, William J. *Best Advice*, 73.

stand a biblical passage or a theological doctrine without pushing toward any particular one.

When the Presbytery of Chicago and its New Church Development team came up with the idea for Wicker Park Grace, they envisioned a "church without walls." That dream has been realized in Wicker Park Grace, and the rest of us have much to learn from this community.

The authentic, enduring Christian communities of tomorrow will simply not have the inclination to split theological hairs nor draw doctrinal lines in the sand. This is not to say that Christians in the once and future church won't need to be biblically and theologically informed. I found my sojourn at Wicker Park Grace extremely biblical, informative, and theologically deep. But part of what all that means in a pluralistic society is that we all accept and even welcome the fact that all theology—including our own carefully crafted belief statements—is constructed by humans, and, therefore, is both limited and time-bound. We must never confuse our words about God—even our best words about God—with God himself. Pastor Nanette made that abundantly and gracefully clear with both her constant references to our "calculated verbal idolatry"—an expression she picked up from a seminary professor—and her open, inviting way of including us all in the theological enterprise.

Despite how the institutional Church has run its affairs in the last 1500 years, the Wicker Park Grace community seems to grasp that the Way of Jesus has never been predicated on right belief nor any doctrinal system. Jesus didn't give people a beliefs test or a creedal statement to sign before they could join his movement, and neither does Pastor Sawyer. Jesus began his relationships with his disciples with three simple words: "Come and see."[19] And what was it, exactly, that Jesus' disciples eventually saw? Was it a sacred list of right beliefs? No! It was a way of life and love that was so compelling, so abundant, that they wanted to live it themselves and share it with everyone they could.

As the institutional Church continues its march of decline, the resurrected communities of Christ that are emerging in places like Wicker Park Grace present us all with an amazing opportunity. It's an opportunity to participate in the theological enterprise rather than offer our reluctant consent to the doctrines and dogmas of our ancestors. It's an opportunity to discuss what our foremothers and fathers struggled to say about God,

19. John 1:39 NIV.

without being asked or required to agree with it all. It's an opportunity to reframe the theological discussion in ways that speak to our hearts and minds today, knowing that our efforts will be just as ephemeral and potentially just as idolatrous as the articulated beliefs with which we were raised.

It is these new or renewed communities like Wicker Park Grace that will, at long last, elevate right living over right belief, which, after all, is the central task of discipleship. And it is discipleship that the institutional Church has mistakenly set aside for hundreds and hundreds of years, while she vigorously pursued the false god of right belief instead. It is discipleship that is now poised to take its rightful place at the forefront of Christianity, and I, for one, can't wait!

I can only imagine what God is ready to do through those communities that are willing to let their biblical interpretations and lists of beliefs be subjugated to the much more concrete and people-centered actions of Jesus. If we can recommit ourselves to living Jesus' Way, not only will we, at long last, more accurately represent the one we call "Lord," but we will also live the kind of compelling and authentic lives others might actually want for themselves.

So it's on to discipleship!

QUESTIONS FOR DISCUSSION

1. Do you make a distinction between "belief" and "faith"? Why or why not?

2. How does the Greek word "pisteuw" challenge your understanding of what it means to be a follower of Jesus?

3. Can you think of a controversy in which your congregation or denomination became embroiled, where the people behind the "issue" were overlooked or demonized?

4. What do you think of the notion that all theology is a "calculated verbal idolatry"?

5. Do you think of yourself as a theologian, someone who is invited into the ongoing conversation about who God is and what God wants from us? Why or why not?

6. Have you or someone you know had an off-putting encounter like Nanette Sawyer had as a child? Share the experience and your/your

friend's response to it. Brainstorm together about how Sawyer's pastor might have handled the young Nanette differently.

7. Jones describes a theological discussion at Wicker Park Grace in which there was "no push for uniformity or agreement," one in which "the whole group sensed that this was a conversation that had no end and no definite answer." Do you have this same sense in the discussions you have in your Bible study groups and Christian education classes? Elaborate.

8. At one point, Pastor Nanette Sawyer says, "Every idea is just that—an idea. I have deep, intense convictions and ideas about God and faith that I am unlikely to let go of. But I won't draw some line around the faith based on them or draw a line between me and another person because of them . . . We don't think of ourselves as having some doctrinal line which one must step over to be a part of us. There is not some fence around our community or some gate one must go through. There is, instead, a center that people go toward, away from, and around. For us, it is our relationships with one another that hold us together." Respond to this quotation, being sure to include whether you see your faith community acting out of this same perspective that Sawyer articulates.

9. Jones notes that folks in his congregation and denomination constantly ask, "Where are all the young people? Why don't any young people come to church anymore?" He then offers his answer, saying, "The answer is that young people are finding communities where there are centers instead of lines, bridges instead of fences, relationships instead of boundaries, and humility instead of arrogance." Do you agree or disagree? Why?

10. Debate Jones' claim that "Jesus didn't give people a beliefs test or a creedal statement to sign before they could join his movement . . . Jesus began his relationships with his disciples with three simple words: "Come and see." If Jones is right, what would the implications be for you, your faith community, and even those outside the Church?

2

Disciple Making

"Non-discipleship is the elephant in the church."[1]

"If we cannot break through to a new vision of faith and discipleship, the real significance and power of the gospel of the kingdom of God can never come into its own."[2]

For at least 500 years, the Christian Church has been all about recruiting church members instead of producing disciples, and, make no mistake, there is an enormous difference between the two. Ever since Martin Luther's camp won the theological battle of the Reformation with "*Sola gratia, Sola Fides*"—Grace alone, faith alone—followers of Christ became convinced that "part of the 'good news' is that one does not have to be a life student of Jesus in order to be a Christian and receive forgiveness of sins."[3] In a gradual progression that some scholars trace back to the Council at Nicea, followers of Christ had gone from *living as* disciples to merely *being* believers. Luther's Reformation contribution seemed to guarantee that the Church henceforth would have a message that would always sell: "Join us and get forgiveness of sins and a ticket to heaven, without ever having to change your life at all!" Of course, this wasn't Luther's intention. He never imagined the ways people would twist his reforming efforts to create an even more dysfunctional Church.

1. Willard, *The Divine Conspiracy*, 301.
2. Ibid., 309.
3. Ibid., 301.

Luther sought to save the church from works righteousness (the belief that we can achieve salvation through our own efforts) and sacerdotalism (the dividing of followers into two distinct classes—clergy and laity—and conferring all authority and privilege upon the clergy). The momentum leading up to the posting of his Ninety-five Theses forced the theological pendulum to swing, and swing it did, with the result that we now find ourselves living in a time when, according to Dallas Willard, "it is almost universally conceded that you can be a Christian without being a disciple."[4] Willard continues: "One can be a professing Christian and a church member in good standing without being a disciple. There is, apparently, no real connection between being a Christian and being a disciple of Jesus."[5]

Jesus preached a gospel of the kingdom of God. He called his followers not simply to *learn about him*, but to *become like him*. He promised his disciples in John 14 that they would actually *do* far greater things than he had done!

Christians are quick to forget that Jesus was a Jewish Rabbi. There was no more rigorous a path than the one to becoming a rabbi—memorizing the entire Torah by age ten, the entire Old Testament by age fourteen, and then apprenticing with one of the top rabbis of the day through the remainder of his teens and into his twenties.

Rabbis in first century Palestine all had their disciples; Jesus was not unique in this regard. And worthy disciples approached their rabbi of choice, not simply because they wanted to know what he knew, but because they desired to do what that particular rabbi did, to be like that rabbi. Dallas Willard, therefore, defines discipleship this way: "A disciple, or apprentice, is simply someone who has decided to be with another person . . . in order to become capable of doing what that person does or become what that person is."[6] "A disciple must be with his rabbi constantly in order to learn from him how to become like him."[7]

One who hangs around most any American church can readily see that what we have in the Christian Church today are not so much disciples of Jesus as fans of Jesus, people interested in learning *about*

4. Willard, 282.

5. Ibid., 291.

6. Willard, 282.

7. Ibid., 291.

Jesus without the genuine intention of actually becoming like him. It is so much easier to fill ourselves with knowledge about Jesus than it is to wrestle with the life-changing call to become like him. This is, no doubt, why Christians have become so obsessed with doctrine and dogma. For if Christ's supposed followers can succeed in making Christian faith solely a matter of correct belief—assenting to the right propositions—we can spend a lifetime, both individually and collectively, arguing what constitutes right belief instead of ever having to bring our lives into line with the Rabbi Jesus' teaching. But as Dallas Willard reminds us, "The narrow gate is not, as so often assumed, doctrinal correctness. The narrow gate is obedience . . . We find many people who seem to be very correct doctrinally but have hearts full of hatred and unforgiveness . . . Those to be trusted are the ones who actually learn to do what Jesus taught was best."[8]

Simply put, Christian discipleship is apprenticeship, the choice to attach oneself to a person whose very life we want to imitate. And there is nothing particularly mysterious or hard to figure out about apprenticeship. "People who are asked whether they are apprentices of a leading politician, musician, lawyer, or screenwriter would not need to think a second to respond . . . The same is all the more true if asked about discipleship to Jesus."[9] "Being a disciple, or apprentice, of Jesus is a quite definite and obvious kind of thing. To make a mystery of it is to misunderstand it. There is no good reason why people should ever be in doubt as to whether they themselves are Jesus' students or not. And the evidence will always be quite clear as to whether any other individual is his student . . ."[10]

But it is a far murkier enterprise to determine whether one is a "Christian," when Christianity is understood as predominantly a matter of internal, intellectual assent to a body of doctrine. For some, the definition of a Christian is one who has "accepted Jesus as Lord and Savior." But what does that mean, exactly? The Apostle Paul might respond referencing Romans 10:9, saying, "Well, if she confesses with her lips that Jesus is Lord and believes it in her heart, she will be saved." But is Christianity strictly about "getting saved?" Can we accurately boil down Jesus' teaching to a one-sentence confession? Can anyone who has read the gospels seriously suggest that Jesus was more concerned with our verbal confes-

---

8. Ibid., 274.

9. Willard, 282.

10. Ibid.

sions of faith than he was with our actions? Consider the following gospel moments:

> Jesus' story of the man with two sons, one of whom says he'll do his father's bidding but doesn't, and another who says he won't do his father's bidding but does. Jesus then asks, "*Which of the two did what his father wanted?*"[11]

> Jesus' parable of The Good Samaritan, which concludes with the following: "*Which of these three do you think was a neighbor to the man who fell into the hands of robbers? . . . Go and do likewise.*"[12]

> The Parable of the Sheep and the Goats in Matthew 25, which Jesus concludes by saying, "*If you've done it unto the least of these, you've done it unto me.*"[13]

> The Parable of the Talents in which Jesus gives three servants three different amounts or talents, and then, in the end, evaluates each servant by what he has done with the gift.[14]

> Jesus' famous teaching in The Sermon on the Mount, in which he says, "*You have heard that it was said, 'Eye for eye, and tooth for tooth.' But I tell you, do not resist an evil person. If someone strikes you on the right cheek, turn to him the other also.*

> *And if someone wants to sue you and take your tunic, let him have your cloak as well. If someone forces you to go one mile, go with him two miles. Give to the one who asks you, and do not turn away from the one who wants to borrow from you.*"[15]

While the Apostle Paul may have been overly concerned with verbal confessions of faith and correct belief as he understood it, Jesus was not. Again and again, Jesus called his disciples to action, to works of love, to *pisteuw* rather than to belief. I am firmly convinced that Jesus has no interest in our debates over dogma and our various doctrinal litmus tests for correct belief. Jesus is much more concerned that his followers be freed up to focus on *doing* what he, himself, did—not just *knowing what* Jesus did or *talking about* what Jesus did—but actually *doing* it. This is discipleship.

11. Matt 21:28–31 NIV.
12. Luke 10:30–37 NIV.
13. Matt 25:31–48 NIV.
14. Matt 25:14–30 NIV.
15. Matt 5:38–42 NIV.

Discipleship will be the curriculum in the post-church communities of the future. Congregations of "believers" who persist in dealing only, or even primarily, with beliefs will continue their precipitous decline toward extinction. Only those communities of disciples who equip and encourage each other to do the things that Jesus did will have the relevance, the respect, and the right to grow and thrive as we move into our very uncertain future.

But "we'll have to come to terms with the fact that we cannot become those who 'hear and do' without specific training for it."[16] Willard claims that what keeps churches from creating authentic disciples is "the absence of effectual programs of training that enable people to do what Jesus said in a regular and efficient manner." Willard goes on to give examples of the kinds of courses and seminars that a community of disciples would regularly offer one another: "How to bless someone who is spitting on you; How to live without purposely indulged lust or covetousness; How to quit condemning the people around you; How to be free of anger and all its complications."[17] We might add to his list "How to give a poor person our shirt and our cloak as well;" "How to give strangers a welcome;" "How to offer one of our empty bedrooms to a street person;" and "How to sell what we have and give the proceeds to the poor."

At this point, I must confess that I have been much more a part of this problem Willard points out than a part of the solution. I am, by many standards, a master teacher with extensive classroom experience, both in churches and several outstanding educational institutions. But as I look at my course offerings in the churches I've served through the years, I see a very troubling pattern: virtually every class I've taught has focused on challenging people's theology and biblical understanding. While at times we may have discussed or read about what it means to live like Jesus, we never once practiced it. Barbara Brown Taylor said it best. "Wisdom is not gained by *knowing* what is right. Wisdom is gained by *practicing* what is right . . . the practice itself will teach them what they need to know."[18]

The radical and vitally necessary transition I am advocating for followers of Jesus— moving from congregations of believers to communities of disciples—will be as difficult for me as it will for the rest of Christendom.

16. Willard, 313.

17. Ibid., 314.

18. Brown Taylor, *An Altar in the World*, 14.

But what excites me and gives me hope in the midst of such a challenge is that I have seen supportive, risk taking, post-Church communities of disciples in places like Wicker Park Grace. My prayer is that we all might, one day, be a part of a community of genuine disciples, so that we can undertake the Bible's tough, world changing challenges together.

My contention is that once individual followers of Christ and entire communities of Christians become disciples—people who not only know what Jesus said and did, but are actually doing it—the entire world will take notice. Christians will go from being reviled to being admired and even emulated. It is also my belief that genuine, authentic discipleship will take away the need for what churches have traditionally called "evangelism." Disciple communities won't need to advertise or promote their ministries, because those who see the behavior of such disciples will want to be a part of their movement. Put another way, "the shock of being dealt with in love and fairness and mercy will certainly change the behavior of others."[19] Think of the priest in *Les Miserables*, who welcomed Jean Valjean into his home despite Valjean's criminal record. Even after Valjean robbed and beat him, this priest came to Valjean's defense before the magistrate. Valjean's shock at this unprecedented, unmerited treatment changed him and set him on an entirely new path. This is the power of discipleship, the power of a life lived in conscious and risk-taking obedience to Christ. While traditional Church Christianity may need to be advertised and marketed to interest others in its offerings, authentic, lived discipleship does not. It is a contagious movement, just as it was in the days that Jesus walked the earth.

But the church of the last 500 years knows next to nothing of discipleship's power, because, for the most part, we haven't witnessed it. It is this failure—the failure to model discipleship and make disciples—more than any other, that is hastening the demise of the Church as we know it. Conversely, it will be communities of genuine disciples that will rise up to replace or reinvigorate the dying Church, and the entire world will be better for it.

What I am most excited about is that time in the not so distant future when communities of Christ followers will support one another in the doing of what Jesus did. None of us can be Christlike on our own. We desperately need a community of support around us, egging us on

19. Willard, 365.

to take the kinds of risks our Rabbi took. I think that communities of Christ in the future will be places of positive peer pressure, where small groups of people will venture into a poor urban area by night, looking for lonely homeless people, armed only with blankets, sandwiches, and a desire to please their master. Future communities of Christ will send a few disciples to the local mayor's office when he is considering enacting a law that pushes poor indigents out of the public park each night. These disciples will quietly and respectfully tell the mayor that, "we want the homeless to be permitted to stay in our public parks, and we intend to reside there too, in solidarity with them, until their right to stay is assured." I long to be a part of a community of disciples where whenever a neighbor loses a spouse or a child, a couple of us go to her and say, "we are here to sit shiva with you," and nothing more is said. I want to serve in a community where, instead of endless committee meetings, we spend our time out in the streets or scouring the newspapers in search of folks who might be hungry, lonely, in prison, bereaved, or oppressed, just so we can support and love them.

As Dallas Willard puts it, "The final step in becoming a disciple is decision. We become a life student of Jesus by deciding . . . It will not just happen. We do not drift into discipleship."[20] So what I am talking about requires intent, the conscious decision to do the very things Christ did. Such behavior is both difficult and contrary to my natural leanings in most every way. For "unless we clearly see the superiority of what we receive as his (Jesus') students over every other thing that might be valued, we cannot succeed in our discipleship to him."[21] But if Christ is the one I've chosen to apprentice with, then it is his nature toward which I must bend my own. All I need is an authentic community willing to undertake this ultimate challenge with me.

It is just such an authentic community of apprentices to Christ that I see emerging in the future, rising up to take the place of a tired and failing Church. It is just such a community of genuine disciples who will silence themselves in favor of acts of love, who will sacrifice their property, their buildings, and all the expenses associated with the traditional Church in exchange for a simple, unencumbered life of generosity and service to the least of these. It is just such a gathering of disciples that will no longer

20. Willard, 297.
21. Ibid., 294.

have time for litmus test questions and doctrinal debates, because they will be too busy doing what their master did. It is just such a missional community that gives away every dollar that it takes in, realizing that the money was never really theirs in the first place.

This is the Church. This is the community of beloved disciples our Rabbi Jesus envisioned and intended to create. How, then did we get so off the track? How did this bureaucratic beast, this life draining, spiritually deadening institution ever get this far? We, his followers, simply weren't willing to risk doing what Jesus did. "No doubt Jesus understood ahead of time that every imaginable way would be tried to avoid simply doing the things he said and knew to be best, and now we see from history and all around us that it has been so."[22]

One of the problems with reading and agreeing with Dallas Willard's definition of discipleship is that it becomes very hard to find a person, much less an entire Christian community actually living the way of Jesus. But after experiencing the power of what is going on at Wicker Park Grace, I was determined to find other communities that could provide an authentic, albeit human, look at living the way of Jesus. One such compelling community of disciples resides in Philadelphia and is known as "The Simple Way." Founder Shane Claiborne is a self-described radical, whose life bears witness to Willard's understanding of discipleship. "I am a radical in the truest sense of the word: an ordinary radical who wants to get at the root of what it means to love, and to get at the root of what has made such a mess of our world."[23]

For Claiborne, being a Christian is about "choosing Jesus and deciding to do something incredibly daring with your life."[24] His attempt to follow in Jesus' footsteps has led him to "the halls of power and the slums of the destitute, amid tax collectors and peasants, and dragged into courtrooms and jail cells."[25]

But Shane's faith hasn't always been so risky and radical. He began his journey going on mission trips and youth retreats, where following Jesus meant going to the foot of the cross and laying one's sins there in order to

22. Willard, 274.
23. Claiborne, *The Irresistible Revolution*, 20.
24. Ibid., 18.
25. Ibid., 19.

be born again. But over time and six to eight born again experiences, Shane got restless, knowing that following Jesus had to mean something more. "I did my devotions, read all the new Christian books and saw the Christian movies, and then vomited information up to friends, small groups, and pastors. But it never had the chance to digest. I had gorged myself on all the products of the Christian industrial complex but was spiritually starving to death."[26] Claiborne and his buddies would later refer to this knowledge based, emotionally charged form of Christianity as "spiritual masturbation," because, while it felt good, it never really gave birth to anything.[27] What Shane really longed for was "to see people who tried to live out the things that Jesus taught."[28] It was getting harder and harder for him to read and study the Bible and then just go about his normal life. He became more and more convinced that anyone who really took Jesus' message to heart and sought to follow it would have his/her world turned upside down. "I know there are people out there who say, 'My life was such a mess. I was drinking, partying, sleeping around . . . and then I met Jesus and my whole life came together.' God bless those people. But me, I had it together. I used to be cool. And then I met Jesus and he wrecked my life. The more I read the gospel, the more it messed me up, turning everything I believed in, valued, and hoped for upside-down."[29]

Claiborne agrees with Mark Twain's assessment that, "It's not the parts of the Bible I don't understand that scare me, but the parts I do understand."[30] In his college years at Eastern University, he was drawn to folks who were taking the way of Jesus seriously. "One night, I was hanging with two buddies who told me they were going down to the city to hang out with their 'homeless friends.' They invited me, and I went . . . again and again. In fact, every chance we got, we would head for the city . . . I was in for a lot of surprises."[31] Eventually, these homeless folks became Claiborne's friends, "some of the most incredible people I'd ever met," he noted. "We would stay up all night and hear each other's stories. It became harder and harder to come back to the comfort of our dorm rooms and leave our

---

26. Ibid., 39.
27. Ibid., 45.
28. Ibid., 46.
29. Claiborne, 41.
30. Ibid., 40.
31. Ibid., 41.

neighbors in their cardboard boxes and to talk about 'loving our neighbors as ourselves' in New Testament classes."[32]

Then came the night when one of Shane's radical friends and fellow students dropped another bomb on his comfortable Christianity. One of them said, "I've been reading Mother Teresa . . . She says that we can't understand the poor until we begin to understand what poverty is like. So tonight we are going to sleep out on the street."[33] Claiborne's jaw dropped, but he went with the others. "Night after night we would head down. The Bible came to life for us there. When we read the Bible on the streets of Philly, it was like watching one of those old-school 3-D movies with the red glasses . . . the words jumped off the pages."[34]

The things Shane saw and experienced on the streets of Philadelphia changed him and his practice of discipleship for good. "I found that I was just as likely to meet God in the sewers of the ghetto as in the halls of academia. I learned more about God from the tears of homeless mothers than any systematic theology ever taught me."[35] Claiborne saw generosity among the homeless that he never expected: a panhandler taking his meager proceeds and sharing them with a dozen of his homeless friends, a hungry woman battling her way through a food line to get a meal that she would take around the corner to another homeless lady who was even hungrier.

Claiborne's faith became about doing the very things Jesus told his disciples to do, practicing the very practices of that first community of disciples. Perhaps the most legendary example of what Shane and The Simple Way community have done in the spirit and the way of Jesus is their creative and risky advocacy of a group of forty homeless families who had taken refuge in an abandoned cathedral in downtown Philly. St. Edward's Cathedral had been closed by the Archdiocese and vacant for years when forty homeless families began using it as their wintertime shelter. When the Archdiocese got wind of this, they gave the families forty-eight hours notice to get out of the building. Claiborne and others from Eastern University jumped into action and enlisted dozens of their cohorts to move into the Cathedral with the homeless families as an act of solidarity and to keep the Archdiocese from taking this heartless action. These

32. Ibid., 48.

33. Claiborne, 48.

34. Ibid.

35. Ibid., 51.

ordinary radicals put up signs and fliers all around their campus that said, "Jesus is getting kicked out of a church in North Philly. Come hear about it. Kea Lounge, 10 p.m. tonight."[36] When the band of disciples showed up at St. Edwards to move in, they told their homeless brothers and sisters, "If they come for you, they'll have to take us too."[37] Not only was this Christlike risk successful—the Archdiocese backed down—but the Eastern University students continued to frequent St. Edward's for impromptu worship and fellowship with their new friends. "It was in St. Edward's that I was born again . . . again," Claiborne said.[38] In this amazing experience, he and others got a taste of the vital, adventurous form of discipleship Jesus intended. "We decided to stop complaining about the church we saw and we set our hearts on becoming the church we dreamed of."[39]

And thus The Simple Way community was born, seeking to flesh out the principles and practices of Jesus rather than merely discussing them. As one of Shane's colleagues said, "I am not a Christian anymore . . . I gave up Christianity in order to follow Jesus."[40] Claiborne and his fellow radicals had had enough of studying Christianity; they were ready to start living it. "I knew we were not going to win the masses to Christianity until we began to live it," he said.[41] One can see Dallas Willard's definition of discipleship—apprenticing one's self to Christ in order to do the things He did—taking root in Claiborne.

The next major chapter in Shane's journey toward authentic discipleship took him to Calcutta, India to see how Mother Teresa and her Sisters of Charity lived out their faith. While there, Shane did everything from visiting folks in the home for the dying to dressing the wounds of lepers. He worked alongside some amazing disciples from all over the world, mostly volunteers, including a German man named Andy. "Andy used to be a wealthy businessman, and then he read the gospel and it 'messed everything up.' He read the part where Jesus commands the disciples to sell everything they have and give it to the poor (Luke 12:33) and he actually did it . . . He sold everything he owned and moved to Calcutta, where

36. Ibid., 57.
37. Ibid., 58.
38. Ibid., 65.
39. Ibid., 64.
40. Ibid., 71.
41. Ibid., 72.

for over ten years, he had spent his life with the poorest of the poor . . . I had gone (to India) in search of Christianity. And I had found it. I had finally met a Christian . . . I was finally seeing a church that was storming the gates of hell itself to save people from its horrors."[42] Claiborne admits that he had gone to Calcutta to "see Christ in Mother Teresa," but he also "found Christ in the lepers, the children, the destitute, and the workers. I even began to recognize that Christ lives in me."[43]

But as profound as this trip to India and to the poorest of the poor had been, Shane, the disciple and community founder, would still have to figure out how to transfer his deepening understanding of church and authentic discipleship to the city of Philadelphia. "When we first started The Simple Way, we thought we'd just live together and love each other. Well, that worked for about a week. We realized we were mostly just reacting against legalistic Christianity and had nothing in terms of formation or discipleship. As a result, we ended up being very sloppy in what we did. Discipleship comes from the same root as discipline, and to be a disciple requires the practice of disciplines."[44]

So early on in his community's history, Shane and his fellow travelers learned about and experimented with the practice of some spiritual disciplines—fasting, praying the daily office, "things like the Jubilee and gleaning laws, special honoring of the poor, the immigrant, the widow are just a few of those ways of being different."[45] They began a network of communities who were interested in this same understanding of discipleship. "We are a part of the New Monasticism that has twelve marks of authentic practice and belief. So if somebody wants to join our movement, he/she can't just "join" by saying so. It's years and years of growing into what we do, practicing what we practice, and living how we live. People that actually want to live with us begin as a novice and then work through different layers of practice and disciplines. Not everyone signs up to live here, but to live here one must live with us in the way we are seeking to live."[46]

Life in The Simple Way is, by design, noticeably different than life in society's mainstream, just as the life Jesus lived with his original disciples

42. Claiborne, 77, 79.

43. Ibid., 89.

44. Shane Claiborne, interview by author, Philadelphia, PA, 21 July 2009.

45. Claiborne, interview.

46. Ibid.

was significantly different than their first century context. "Part of what we have to do as followers of Jesus is leave some things in order to gain other things. We leave much of the clutter, routine, and predictability behind, because they don't give life to ourselves or anyone else. We say 'no' to a lot of meetings, other activities, and even programs that often become routine and take away our ability to live in the moment, to be interrupted, and to live like Jesus did."[47]

I pushed Shane on this point, wanting to know how his community maintains spontaneity and the flexibility to be interrupted. "We have to make space for that relational, neighborhood stuff. This is why we don't have full time jobs here, or we wouldn't have the time to do all the simple, great stuff we do. We've gotten rid of T.V. in our place. We play with the neighborhood kids, whether it's sidewalk chalk or juggling or some made-up game. We nurture and create room for our imaginations."[48] Claiborne rooted this stripped down, spontaneous approach to living in the person of Jesus.

"When we look at Jesus, we see he was always getting interrupted, and that's where the miracles take place."[49]

When I asked Shane for some sample miracle stories from his community, I expected some huge, supernatural tales. What I got instead were very ordinary stories of daily living Jesus style.

> We had a family here with their kids, raising them on the block. That couple always brought their kids to our house, saying, 'We want them to grow up with different values than we grew up with. Just because someone smells, we don't want our kids to be afraid of them.' So this one day, Alexa, their daughter, who was about two or three at the time, was with them at the house, and at one point ran up to a homeless guest and jumped straight into his lap. The man immediately pushed her away and apologized to her parents, as if to say, 'I'm sure you don't want *me* to touch your daughter.' But Alexa's parents said, 'Sure we do! Hold her! We want you to!' You should have seen what their response did to this homeless man! They made him feel alive again. This man had probably not held or been allowed to touch anyone for who knows how long. This was a huge moment for him.

47. Ibid.
48. Claiborne, interview.
49. Ibid.

Only by minimizing the typical programmatic and highly scheduled aspects of more traditional churches has The Simple Way created an environment where so many simple miracles can occur. "I like what Dorothy Day said," Shane added. 'We must create an environment where it's easier for people to be good.' That's what we try to do here. We've had to resist so much of what the Church does so that we are still able to do what Mother Teresa said—'to do simple, ordinary things with extraordinary love' instead of trying to do great big things."[50]

While Claiborne's community may seem radical and somehow standing in opposition to what we think of as Church, he is careful to claim a deep and abiding connection to the larger institution. "From the beginning, God has been forming a people, people who live differently from the patterns of the world around them, not just for themselves, but to show the world what a society of love looks like and to woo the rest of the world toward God. The whole biblical story is a love story, God loving us even in our running away."[51] If there is a critique of the traditional church in Claiborne's work, it comes in pointing out the vital distinction between a doing-oriented discipleship and a belief-based one. "Jesus doesn't ask us to sign up to a list of doctrines or beliefs; he invites us to join a movement. Everything God hoped Israel to be was fulfilled in Jesus, and we are now to be God's hands and feet in the world."[52]

But don't let the intensity of action or the monastic discipline of The Simple Way fool you. There is a genuine, palpable joy present in this inner city Philadelphia community; some might even call it playfulness. "A lot of what we choose in the more typical patterns of the world doesn't bring us true joy or abundant life. Living with people the way we do is great! Jesus is calling us to life to the fullest, for ourselves and others! One thing a lot of liberals and conservatives have in common is they've lost their joy. They can't even laugh, and that's the devil's goal: to rob our joy. As Emma Goldman said, 'If I can't dance, then it's not my revolution.'"[53]

Shane's months with Mother Teresa enabled him to see her genuine joy in the very midst of horrific suffering. "There's a story of some reporter who followed Mother Teresa around for awhile and eventually said to

50. Claiborne, interview.

51. Ibid.

52. Ibid.

53. Claiborne, interview.

her, 'I couldn't do what you do for a million dollars.' Mother Teresa said, 'Me neither.'[54] Her point was that there is no dollar amount that could enhance the joy and satisfaction she felt ministering to the poorest of the poor. One senses that same satisfaction and joy in Shane Claiborne.

The Simple Way doesn't seek to walk and live as disciples of Jesus in isolation. Claiborne constantly references the network of communities with which his particular one interacts. Camden Community House is one such community that lives in dialogue and fellowship with The Simple Way. Founded by Shane's long-time friend and the co-author of *Jesus for President,* Chris Haw, Camden Community House is in its sixth year. Haw's desire to actually follow Jesus as an apprentice is what led him to move into a poor, crime-ridden, urban neighborhood in Camden, New Jersey. He and his wife procured an abandoned house and began to work on it, making it their home. Another couple followed suit in the same triangular block. While so many individuals and churches are moving out of neighborhoods like this one, Chris's understanding of discipleship led him to move in to one.

> Ours is a ministry against fear, especially when people first join us down here. One of our houses is right by a liquor store, where recently a woman was severely beaten by four guys. We hear gunshots fairly regularly, and my wife told me the other day that she is propositioned for sex on a daily basis around here. There are no easy solutions that present themselves when dealing with this kind of darkness. But we have dinner together and talk about it, sharing in what some have called 'the fellowship of the suffering.' Sure it's a challenge living here, surrounded by the darkness of the world. We are, in a sense, missionaries in this neighborhood.[55]

Clearly, Haw and the folks at Camden Community House believe that Jesus would have been in a neighborhood like theirs, making it better, working toward healing and reconciliation. As Jesus' apprentices, they are setting out to do what their master did.

But the Camden House Community is not in existence simply to suffer as martyrs. "There are significant pluses to living in a neighborhood that's falling apart," Haw noted. "Creativity beckons you everywhere you look around here. I'm a carpenter and when I see scraps of discarded wood outside abandoned buildings, I gather them up and make a table

---

54. Ibid.

55. Chris Haw, interview by author, Camden, NJ, August 16, 2009.

or something out of it. You should see some of the gardens we've planted where old abandoned houses and lots were. We're growing amazing stuff and creating some real beauty here."[56] Haw also talked about the social benefits of living with and around members of his intentional community. "By living in this environment and so close to one another, we are able to share a closeness that isn't possible in a church setting where you see each other once or twice a week for an hour or so."[57] A vital part of Camden Community House's life together is committed involvement in an existing Catholic parish rooted right in their neighborhood. "There are quite a few older folks in this small church, and getting to eat, worship, and hang out with them at each other's homes has been great and enriching for us."[58] Perhaps most telling of all is the fact that after only six years of the three or four houses worth of Camden Community House members moving in, "the block has a cared for look and feel to it. There's far less drug traffic and prostitution around here than before we moved in. There's palpable hope as well."[59]

Such "palpable hope" for this section of Camden could never have resulted from mere conversations between Christians or Bible studies in some church basement, though those were and still are foundational parts of this amazing community as it has taken shape. At some point, these followers of Jesus actually had to choose what Haw calls "downward mobility," voluntarily entering the underclass, and not just for a week-long mission trip, but as their permanent residence.[60] But Haw is quick to clarify that he doesn't seek to glorify or glamorize downward mobility when so many of God's children are struggling so mightily to get out of poverty. "It's not that downward mobility is some sort of pre-requisite for being a part of our community. For us, it is discipleship to Jesus that is the main theme of our lives, and we are willing to be held accountable to that intention."[61]

In my interactions with both The Simple Way and Camden Community House, I felt like I was seeing Jesus in the modern world. I also found folks who are seeking to live out Dallas Willard's understand-

56. Haw, interview.

57. Ibid.

58. Haw, interview.

59. Ibid.

60. Ibid.

61. Ibid.

ing of discipleship; they are actually getting on the bike and riding it. The people in these communities seem to grasp that when Jesus said things like, "Whoever wants to be my disciple must deny themselves and take up their cross daily and follow me," or "sell your possessions and give to the poor . . . and come follow me," he actually meant them.[62]

Thanks be to God that there are Christians taking the call and cost of discipleship seriously enough to change their lives. It is in and through such communities as Camden Community House, The Simple Way, and Wicker Park Grace that God's kingdom is coming and His will is being done on earth. I long to be a part of such a community, and I also pray that I might become the kind of disciple that Claiborne and Haw are becoming. It isn't easy work, living as a true disciple. In fact, it's pretty risky, too risky for most church folk. But when we're a part of a community of disciples, we stand a much better chance of becoming disciples ourselves. And so we turn our attention to how a community can help us take Christlike risks, the risks that apprentices of Jesus are called to take.

QUESTIONS FOR DISCUSSION

1. "A disciple, or apprentice, is simply someone who has decided to be with another person . . . in order to become capable of doing what that person does or become what that person is . . . A disciple must be with his rabbi constantly in order to learn from him how to become like him." Discuss Dallas Willard's definition of a disciple. How have you understood discipleship throughout your Christian journey?

2. Wrestle with Jones' assertions that, "What we have in the Christian Church today are not so much disciples of Jesus as fans of Jesus, people interested in learning *about* Jesus without the genuine intention of actually becoming like him. It is so much easier to fill ourselves with knowledge about Jesus than it is to wrestle with the life-changing call to become like him." Does your faith community spend more time learning about Jesus or working to become like him? How do you know?

3. Dallas Willard asserts that, "The final step in becoming a disciple is decision. We become a life student of Jesus by deciding . . . It will not just happen. We do not drift into discipleship." Do you agree

---

62. Luke 9:23, Matt 19:21.

or disagree? What has been your experience of how people become genuine disciples who live in the Way of Jesus?

4. "I am firmly convinced that Jesus has no interest in our debates over dogma and our various doctrinal litmus tests for correct belief. Jesus is much more concerned that his followers be freed up to focus on *doing* what he, himself, did—not just *knowing what* Jesus did or *talking about* what Jesus did—but actually *doing* it. This is discipleship." Do you agree with Jones here? Why or why not?

5. Willard claims that what keeps churches from creating authentic disciples is "the absence of effectual programs of training that enable people to do what Jesus said in a regular and efficient manner." Has your faith community offered any training courses that have helped you actually do the things Jesus did? Do you think any of Willard's suggested courses would be well received in your congregation? Why or why not?

6. Consider renting the film Les Miserables starring Liam Nieson and viewing the first 15 minutes as a group. Discuss the ways the Catholic priest treats Jean Valjean. Is this priest a disciple as Willard defines one? What are the risks and dangers inherent in doing what Jesus did?

7. Reread the story of St. Edward's Cathedral and how the group of Eastern University students moved in with the homeless community there. Was this an act of discipleship? Why or why not? Has your community of faith ever done anything like this? If not, why not?

3

Communities of Risk and Adventure

Each of us is born with two contradictory sets of instructions; a conserva-
tive tendency, made up of instincts for self-preservation, self-aggrandize-
ment, and saving energy, and an expansive tendency made up of instincts
for exploring, for enjoying novelty and risk—the curiosity that leads to
creativity belongs to this set. We need both of these programs. But whereas
the first tendency requires little encouragement or support from the outside
to motivate behavior, the second can wilt if it is not cultivated. If too few
opportunities for curiosity are available, if too many obstacles are placed
in the way of risk and exploration, the motivation to engage in creative
behavior is easily extinguished.[1]

—Mihaly Csikszentmihalyi

IF THERE'S ONE THING I've learned about myself in 48 years, it's that I'm
not much of a risk taker. And if there's one thing I've learned about
Jesus of Nazareth in over 30 years of studying his life, it's that he and those
who became his disciples were huge risk takers. So where does that leave
me as one who claims to follow and serve Jesus?

For me to have any hope of growing into Christlikeness, I'm going to
need the support and encouragement of others who are trying to take the
kind of risks Jesus and his followers took. My twisting, turning spiritual
journey included fifteen years completely divorced from the Church. This
split occurred after seminary and after serving as a pastor for several years.
I'd had enough—too much, actually—of church politics and infighting. I
found the church not only to be no better than any other organization in

---

1. Mihaly Csikszentmihalyi, *Creativity: Flow and the Psychology of Discovery and
Invention*, quoted in Doug Pagitt and Tony Jones, *An Emergent Manifesto of Hope* (Grand
Rapids: Baker Books, 2007), 70.

terms of how people treated one another, but actually worse. I could go on and on about all that's wrong with this very human institution that started out as Christ's *ecclesia*. But the truth is, I still need a Christian community, an *ecclesia* with all its flaws, if I am ever to become more Christlike. And I don't believe that I am alone in this need.

By now it should be abundantly clear that when I talk about being Christlike, I'm talking about actually *doing* what Jesus did, not just talking about it or solidifying some belief system around it. I can believe in or have faith in Jesus and in the scriptures just fine on my own. During my fifteen-year hiatus from any Christian community, I never once doubted the existence of God, the power of Christ's resurrection, nor anything else in the realm of belief. But the living of my life—my practice of Jesus' way— was an entirely different story. On my own for this decade and a half, I didn't take the risks that Jesus calls his disciples to take: the risky sharing of my financial resources, the risky loving of outcasts and strangers, the risky welcoming of the homeless and AIDS victims, or the risky visiting of the prisoner and the hospice patient. All these central actions of a true disciple were utterly absent from my life when I was doing Christianity solo. Why? Because I'm not a risk taker by nature, and virtually every-thing Jesus calls his followers to do is risky.

In case you're not accustomed to thinking of Christian discipleship as risky business, let's review a small sampling of some of the difficult challenges to which Jesus called his disciples.

"Calling the Twelve to him, Jesus began to send them out two by two and gave them authority over evil spirits. These were his instructions: 'Take nothing for the journey except a staff—no bread, no bag, no money in your belts. Wear sandals but not an extra shirt. Whenever you enter a house, stay there until you leave that town. And if any place will not welcome you or listen to you, shake the dust off your feet when you leave, as a testimony against them.'"[2]

In John 4, Jesus takes the unprecedented and unlawful step of enter-ing Samaria, a land considered unclean and capable of corrupting a Jew. Jesus takes the twelve with him into Samaria, making them extremely uncomfortable, frightened, and angry, not to mention "unclean." To make matters worse, Jesus sits down and has a lengthy, public conversation with a woman, which is also forbidden under Jewish law. The fact that this

2. Mark 6:7–11 NIV.

woman has been married five times and is now living with a sixth makes Jesus' actions here utterly unbearable for his followers.[3]

In all of the gospel narratives, Jesus sends the twelve out not only to preach and teach, but to heal and cast out demons as well. In Mark 9, the disciples try to heal a boy who has what sounds like epilepsy, but they fail. Jesus comes upon the scene and the father of the sick boy says, "Teacher, I brought you my son, who is possessed by a spirit that has robbed him of speech. Whenever it seizes him, it throws him to the ground. He foams at the mouth, gnashes his teeth, and becomes rigid. I asked your disciples to drive out the spirit, but they could not." Jesus then goes on to reprimand the disciples publicly for failing in their healing attempt, saying, "You unbelieving generation, how long shall I put up with you?"[4]

In several of the gospel accounts of Jesus' triumphal entry, the story begins with Jesus asking a couple of his disciples to go into a nearby village and essentially steal someone else's colt. "Go to the village ahead of you, and as you enter it, you will find a colt tied there, which no one has ever ridden. Untie it and bring it here. If anyone asks you, 'Why are your untying it?' say, 'The Lord needs it.'"[5] Even though the story turns out well for those who run this strange errand, it must have been a huge and uncomfortable risk for them. Imagine doing something similar today.

The Book of Acts gives us a glimpse of the early church in its infancy. The fourth chapter demonstrates the high and all-consuming calling of being a disciple in those days. In our day and age, it has become extremely rare for a follower of Christ to live up to the tithe, offering 10% of his earnings to the church community. But in Acts 4 we read, "No one claimed that any of their possessions was their own, but they shared everything they had . . . there were no needy persons among them. For from time to time those who owned land or houses sold them, brought the money from the sales, and put it at the apostles' feet, and it was distributed to anyone who had need."[6]

And finally, this excerpt from Jesus' famous Sermon on the Mount further emphasizes the incredible risks to which our Lord calls us: "Love your enemies, do good to those who hate you, bless those who curse

---

3. John 4:4–27 NIV.

4. Mark 9:15–19 NIV.

5. Luke 19:29–34 NIV.

6. Acts 4:32–35 NIV.

you. If someone slaps you on one cheek, turn and offer the other also. If someone takes your coat, offer him your shirt as well. Give to everyone who asks you, and if anyone takes what belongs to you, do not demand it back."[7]

Being an apprentice to Jesus is risky business, even dangerous at times. So what happens when one who is generally afraid of risks, as I am, joins up with today's institutional Church? I get affirmed in my desire to keep the boat from rocking, in my commitment to protect the status quo, and in my fear-based tendency to do or say nothing that feels remotely risky. In short, I become a part of the unconscious conspiracy to turn Christianity into niceness, into a force protecting the status quo instead of challenging it. Jesus was not about any of these things. His call to those who would be his disciples was a call to challenge the status quo of religiosity at every turn. Being a follower of Jesus was and is extremely risky business.

Future communities of Christ followers will be communities of risk. They will invite wimps like me to venture outside of our comfort zones to where genuine discipleship is forged. I can imagine getting a phone call from my fellow disciples in a resurrection community someday saying, "Toby, a bunch of us are going over to the AIDS clinic to hang out for the day. Come with us!" Or "A few of us are going to sit shiva with John, who lost his wife last night. Come with us." Or "It's Friday night and we're going down to the viaduct where the homeless folks live. We're taking sandwiches and guitars just to hang out. We'll pick you up on our way." Or "Tomorrow afternoon is when I visit a couple guys at the state prison. I'd love for you to come along and see what it's all about." Or even "We just found out that Steve and Martha lost their jobs and their health insurance. Martha is six months pregnant and they're really panicked. We're looking for people who will join us in covering their insurance and food costs until they can find new jobs and get back on their feet. Are you in?"

Brian McLaren puts it this way: "Most of the truly important skills we learn in life come through training, practice, and tradition or community . . . And the community of people who teach us the practices we could define as a *community of practice* . . . I think this is what happens to all of us when we feel a pull toward God . . . We set out to become someone we can't currently be simply by deciding or trying, and we do so by taking on practices in a community that carries the tradition that has won our hearts."[8]

7. Luke 6:27–31, NIV.

8. McLaren, Finding Our Way Again, 80–83.

McLaren is spot on here, and I am compelled to borrow his wonderful phrase "a community of practice." I have carefully avoided using the word "church" when talking about this new kind of community I envision replacing the dying institution we have come to think of as "church." Perhaps McLaren's innovative term is precisely the one for which I've been searching. It captures the critical notion that to get better at living the way Jesus lived requires both practice and the constant support of a community. Mihaly Csikszentmahalyi said essentially the same thing about what he called our "expansive tendency," warning that the creative and exploratory aspects of our nature will "wilt if not cultivated."[9]

I experienced the power of a community of practice when I spent a week at Glide Memorial United Methodist Church in San Francisco's Tenderloin district. Far and away the most inclusive and diverse community of Christ followers I've ever seen, Glide has lived in Christlike risk since the early 1960's. Because of Glide's radical hospitality and multi-pronged approach to serving the poorest of the poor, a day at Glide means rubbing elbows and sharing meals with the homeless, the mentally ill, crack addicts, and people suffering from every other malady that extreme and chronic poverty can foist upon them.

After just four days of sojourning with this community in all its diversity, I was walking back to my hotel at about 10:30 in the evening, when I was approached by a young, homeless man. He asked me for money to get some food. This man's request was nothing new to me. I've been through this exact scene countless times, and my responses have ranged from a quick and uncomfortable "Sorry" uttered without eye contact, to an equally rapid and awkward search for spare change, to a more sincere, humanely paced, albeit brief conversation without money changing hands. But on this night, without the slightest hesitation or discomfort, I stopped, looked this bearded gentleman in the eye, and asked, "What are you hungry for?" He said, "Burger King," and I asked him where the nearest one was. He gestured up the street with his head, and I said, "Burger King it is." And off we went. I asked him his name and we talked our way up the block until we entered Burger King. He ordered a Number Seven Value Meal, and I paid the bill. We then picked out a table for two and spent the next half hour together in conversation.

9. Csikszentmihalyi, 70.

I couldn't help noticing how relaxed and unafraid I was. Even though this action represented a huge and unprecedented risk for me, the week I had spent immersed in a community of practice, one that placed such an emphasis on treating everyone as a brother or sister, empowered me to go where I had not gone before. My experience in the Glide community, in Csikszentmihalyi's words, cultivated my motivation and ability to engage in creative behavior and I enjoyed its novelty and risk.[10] It was, indeed, a beautiful experience.

I am completely convinced that communities of practice like Glide will arise to take the place of the dying or at least dysfunctional Church. These resurrection communities will not simply be worshiping communities or gathering communities, nor even communities of believers. They will be practicing communities, disciples in training, pushing the envelope, taking the same risks in the name of Jesus that the original twelve took back in Galilee.

How exciting! Is there anyone who would not be transformed by participation in such a community of practice? What might worship be like in such a community? What about Bible Study or fellowship? Can you imagine the energy, the stories, and the emotional intensity of such a community? Would such a community of practice have any need whatsoever for an evangelism committee or a marketing campaign? Surely not, for the regular and consistent action of the community would create a "come and see" culture like the one Jesus himself initiated two millennia ago.

Communities of practice would also be far less susceptible to the charge of being hypocritical or self-serving than today's church is. They wouldn't be so apt to get bogged down in theological debates, given their intense focus on Christlike action. And think of how appealing such faith communities would be to the younger generations! The raw adventure and constant adrenaline rush of authentic discipleship lived out in the streets and alleys would be irresistible to America's youth. Such a focus on Christlike action might also re-inspire older Americans as they move into a new stage of their lives and spiritual journeys.

∾

My visit to Solomon's Porch up in Minneapolis, Minnesota in May of 2009 gave me a concrete look at a genuine community of risk. Now in their tenth year of existence, this unusual community lives on the edge of

10. Csikszentmihalyi, 70.

its own extinction. And if their pastor Doug Pagitt has his way, they will continue to do so.

"I think that the biggest threat to any Christian community is its sustainability — the drive to see to it that it will exist forever. Why would any of us want to exist forever?" Pagitt asked. "We should only be around as long as we're doing things that allow us to be a blessing to the world. At Solomon's Porch, we're constantly deciding things and doing things that could mean the end of us."[11]

In their ten years, the people of Solomon's Porch have had to move four different times to four distinct neighborhoods within Minneapolis. When a church doesn't own its own space, it can find itself homeless in fairly short order. While that sort of economic vulnerability could be too much for many traditional congregations to handle, most of the folks at Solomon's Porch have embraced it as a part of their life together.

"Our moves have really been whole community events, involving remodeling the new venue ourselves before moving in. These relocations have bound us together and have cultivated and deepened a lot of relationships," said Luke Hillestad, one of the many artists who call Solomon's Porch home.[12]

But Ben Johnson, a lead musician for Solomon's Porch, recalls the downside of their many moves. "At one point, the guys in the band had decided to build a studio within our facility at the time. Right when we had finished and were about to get it up and running, we found out we were moving, and the new place didn't have the appropriate space for a studio."[13]

The decisions and actions the Porch takes, Doug believes, are all temporary and conditional, simply what's right or best at that particular moment in time. And he lives comfortably within that vulnerability. "I'm fine with understanding all our decisions as temporary. When we make a decision, we're pretty much deciding to do that particular thing for another year. And after that, nobody really knows how our decisions will pan out. I certainly don't and that's fine. But we'll figure it out together. And as for the very real risk of us not being around in a year or two, even that doesn't need to be a prohibitive one," Pagitt concluded.[14]

11. Doug Pagitt, interview by author, tape recording, Minneapolis, MN., 4 May, 2009.

12. Luke Hillestad, interview by author, tape recording, Minneapolis, MN., 5 May, 2009.

13. Ben Johnson, interview by author, tape recording, Minneapolis, MN., 4 May, 2009.

14. Pagitt, interview.

This kind of vulnerability, risk, and openness to an uncertain future seems to be woven into the fabric of Solomon's Porch and of Pagitt himself. During the May 3, 2009 worship gathering, he introduced the biblical celebration of Pentecost, speaking of it as a time of great possibility and hope, but also a time of tremendous fear and uncertainty for the disciples. God pouring his spirit out upon the people and sending them out in different directions to be a blessing to others was an exciting new start. But no one knew where all this would lead. In this context, Pagitt and the leaders of Solomon's Porch sought to link the Bible's Pentecost story with their own unfolding story as a community. Pagitt announced in worship that in the twelve weeks following Pentecost, the Solomon's Porch community would cease their regular and wildly successful Sunday evening gatherings. They would, instead, enter a time of discernment to reexamine their shape, structure, and organization in order to evaluate whether what they're doing and how they're doing it is still beneficial to the world. They would also take a serious look at the opportunity they've been offered to purchase the building they've been meeting in for the past few years.

As a visitor to the Porch, I was shocked by this announcement. I had been completely wowed by what had become their status quo. Their worship vibe was powerful, relaxed, and unlike anything I'd ever experienced. The make up of their community—mostly twenty and thirty something's—is precisely what most of the rest of us are seeking to cultivate in our churches but can't seem to achieve. Clearly, this is a congregation that is meaningfully and positively involved in the world throughout the rest of the week through things like their campaign to end human trafficking and their partnership in San Juan, Guatemala. To me, Solomon's Porch was not only already way outside the box, but was truly a difference making and exemplary community, as edgy as I could even imagine. Yet here they were, voluntarily entering a period of discernment to consider whether they had become complacent or were somehow stagnating!

When I asked Pagitt about this decision over coffee, he smiled and said, "Yeah, I know. People say to me, 'Every time we get to a point of relative stability, you ramp it up and throw it all off kilter.' But that's a part of my job. People in general, and Christian organizations in particular, are always trying to avoid vulnerability. But we're *supposed* to be vulnerable!" Pagitt chuckled, sipped his coffee, and went on. "Most people have it as a part of their ecclesiology that their church must always exist. No we don't! Churches are temporary social organisms. I ask the folks here at the Porch all the time, 'Should we still exist?' and 'Should we exist as we currently are?' And again, it all comes down to whether or not we are still doing the kinds of things that bless the world."[15]

Luke Hillestad, an artist and leader in the Solomon's Porch community, added, "Doug is very consistent in pushing us away from any patterns or thoughtless routines. We're always remaking things at Solomon's Porch."[16]

There's an uncanny humility in Pagitt and in his assessment of this amazing community he birthed. He harbors no illusions that the world somehow stands or falls on whether Solomon's Porch survives or not. He compared their situation to a clip he saw of Bruce Springsteen and the East Street Band during their "Magic" tour in 2008.

> Springsteen had gathered the band together backstage just before the curtain came up, and he said, 'What we're about to go out and do is the thing we were created to do and the most important thing we can do right now. And it doesn't matter at all.' And I think what he meant was that this one particular concert didn't matter in the total scheme of who and what the band has been about all these years. But it was still where they were at that one moment in time, and so it deserved their all. That's how I feel about the tension we live in at Solomon's Porch. I know that what we're doing at any point in time is not at the core of what this thing (Solomon's Porch) is. But we still do it as best we can.[17]

Pagitt spent a significant amount of time in more traditional settings before starting Solomon's Porch in 1998. He believes that denominational churches all have risk, humility, and vulnerability in their histories, but have "forgotten where they've been," and lost touch with those chapters in their history.[18] "Where local congregations lose their way is that they forget who they were at the beginning, when they were struggling and risking and trying to make all this stuff happen. And again, it's that achievement of 'sustainability' that is the curse, when congregations stop moving, stop progressing, stop risking and recognizing what they're here for. It is part of my job at Solomon's Porch to never let us get to that

---

15. Pagitt, interview.

16. L. Hillestad, interview.

17. Pagitt, interview.

18. Pagitt, interview.

point of sustainability. We've got to keep moving and changing. It's in the Emergent DNA."[19]

I witnessed one such change and risk the Sunday I was at Solomon's Porch. As a part of the worship gathering, Solomon's Porch makes a practice of having individuals within their community tell their own stories. On that first Sunday in May of 2009, a middle-aged man came to the center to share his journey, from his childhood in Texas to his more recent move to Minneapolis. He spoke of his sexual orientation, which he'd known, even in childhood, to be homosexual. But he knew he couldn't allow himself to be "that way" in Texas, in his family, and in the church, and so he put that part of himself "on a shelf." He eventually got married, had a son, and went on living the heterosexual lie as best he could for as long as he could, including attending several camps and programs aimed at "curing" his homosexuality. In the past year, he decided to come out, a risk that cost him dearly—both his marriage and his relationship with his son.

Having been at Solomon's Porch for about eight months, he had sat and listened to the stories of other participants. He began to feel the desire to tell his own. He approached some of the leaders at Solomon's Porch expressing this desire, saying that he'd come to trust this community and to believe in the genuine friendships he'd developed in his time there.

Doug told me afterwards that this risky situation was one they really weren't prepared for and hadn't anticipated.

> We had never really dealt with the question of homosexuality in our community. It's not that we were avoiding it; it just hadn't come up in any real, personal way in our ten years. This gentleman came to our community eight months ago pretty much like everyone else has and for many of the same reasons. When he expressed a desire to share this part of his story with us, we felt like we wanted to honor his desire. It wasn't like we set out to take this risk—even though it was a significant risk. Half our congregation could have been offended or found his story too much for them. Lots of folks could have left our community. But we risked it and you saw what happened.[20]

What happened was that people applauded his story and affirmed his place in the Solomon's Porch community.

19. Ibid.
20. Pagitt, interview.

To me, this story says so much about Solomon's Porch and the way a community of disciples empowers people to take risks, stretching themselves beyond a previous comfort zone. For the gay man, it was his real experience of community at Solomon's Porch—and particularly his listening as others told their stories—that empowered him to risk telling his own. For the larger community, it was their healing web of relationships with this man as a part of their community that empowered them to risk offering him the platform to tell his story. Loving community emboldens us to risk doing the work of love and compassion.

Kristi Murchie, a regular at Solomon's Porch, who happened to be sitting on the same couch with me that night, put it this way: "We keep coming back to the Porch because it engages both our hearts and our minds. This community is open to see the many ways in which the Spirit moves, not limiting itself to any one tradition, but honoring all of us who bring our own traditions with us when we come here. We feel there is space at Solomon's Porch for all to have a voice, and the community is open to change as new voices are being added to our collective whole all the time."[21]

I witnessed several other risks that the Solomon's Porch community has embraced as well. They have a long-term partnership in Guatemala with the village of San Juan. Eighteen of their participants recently returned from a week of building houses and lining up sponsorships for thirty Guatemalan children, so those children could attend school for another year. "Part of what we do is open people's per-view and help them see and care about parts or aspects of the world they haven't really considered before," Pagitt explained.[22] Solomon's Porch folks who didn't go on the trip had the opportunity to participate by helping fund the trip or by getting the thirty children sponsored for another year. For those who actually traveled, the experience definitely shook up their faith and their understanding of the world in some unanticipated ways.

Michelle Hillestad, the spouse of Luke who was introduced earlier, went on one of these trips seven years ago when she was only eighteen.

> I'd been on 'mission trips' before with other groups whose purpose was to 'evangelize the natives.' So just going to another developing nation didn't feel like some big risk to me. But those other trips were sort of hit and run. We dropped in, did our thing, and left.

21. Kristi Murchie. interview by author, tape recording, Minneapolis, MN., 3 May, 2009.

22. Pagitt, interview.

The Solomon's Porch trip was more wholistic in its intentions. Our particular trip was just one part of a long-term relationship we have with the San Juan community, which means there was much more of a give and take. I came back with a lot of questions, and I still wrestle with what this experience means. Did we really do the San Juan community any long-term good? Were we as sensitive to their needs as we should have been? I mean, we have established life-long relationships with these Mayans who live in a remote mountain village. Some of them still think of me as family. There's a lot of ongoing responsibility in that.[23]

While Michelle's husband Luke hasn't yet been to Guatemala, he spoke of the daily risks he has experienced living in intentional community with Solomon's Porch.

We spend so much time with each other in every conceivable setting. Many participants are here three to four times a week. I'm here pretty much every day, and most every aspect of my life is shared with the folks from the Porch. This community teaches us to be truly vulnerable with each other. It's not like you can just put on some Sunday vibe for each other for that one hour a week you're together. Here it's more like living together; you wind up in each other's presence and space when you really haven't had a chance to be guarded. So there are real relational risks that one takes within this community. We also share our vocations with each other. If something needs to get done around here, we ask the person with that particular skill to get it done. We all do what we can to help each other get off the ground vocationally as well. I've been a painter for a long time and always wanted to earn my living that way. But instead I'd always get some nine to five job and then paint all night. When I came here, people really encouraged me to quit my job and go for it as a painter. Some bought work and everyone really supported me through the risk.[24]

One of Hillestad's fellow artists at the Porch is singer/songwriter Ben Johnson. Ben has been a partner with Pagitt through all ten years of this risky experiment in Christian community. "When we started this thing, Doug was the prophet and I was the poet. We decided very early on that we would do all original music in our gatherings, and that, of course, is a very vulnerable thing," Johnson admitted. "It's not just that it's my

23. Michelle Hillestad, interview by author, tape recording, Minneapolis, MN., 5 May, 2009.

24. L. Hillestad, interview.

own songs I'm doing, but that lots of times they're truly unfinished. Some of the songs actually come about right then and there, out of something we're wrestling with or trying to get a handle on."[25]

Johnson, who is an accomplished, professional musician, involved in both opera and classical performance in the Minneapolis area, acknowledged that doing his own music in the context of the Solomon's Porch community is unlike anything he's ever done.

> I've always believed that any group of people will have their own music, stuff that not only reflects but affects their thoughts and their lives. In trying to be a kind of voice for this community, I'm constantly trying to develop a sense of what resonates with what's going on with us as a community and what will move us somewhere. So in a lot of ways, it's not just about me, and yet I find that I'm often able to write about where I am at any particular point in time and have that really speak to the community as well.[26]

As for the risks Solomon Porch has enabled him to take, Johnson said,

> The other song writers and I take risks in saying some pretty subversive things in our tunes, and here we feel supported in that. One of the songs we did when you were with us (Sunday, May 3, 2009) includes the line, 'knowing more won't teach the blind to see.' Or in our Alleluiah response we say, 'Alleluiah, sing it to ya, Hope it moves ya to make it right.'[27]

Even Johnson's more beautiful, prayerful songs contain jabs like these that push the participant to turn faith into risky action that matters and makes a difference in the world.

When asked about the seemingly endless change at Solomon's porch, Johnson chuckled. "We've been through a lot in ten years together. At first, Doug and I were the only paid staff in the community. We've added staff since and had folks come and go. But one thing we've always held to is that we always want to let everyone have his/her say around here. We've always been willing to sacrifice structures in order to let the Spirit speak."[28]

---

25. Ben Johnson, interview.

26. Johnson, interview.

27. Ibid.

28. Ibid.

The longer I sojourned at Solomon's Porch, the more I began to see that "letting the Spirit speak" and "letting everyone have his/her say" are absolutely crucial values that figure into everything this community does. Even in aspects of ministry that might traditionally be thought of as more individual endeavors, the Porch operates in more communal ways, gathering and listening to one another.

Pagitt's sermon preparation is a prime example. Rather than withdrawing to a quiet place to prepare his Sunday messages in isolation, Doug begins by gathering a dozen or so participants from the community to read and talk about the scripture passage for the upcoming week. This Bible discussion happens every Tuesday night at 7:30 and represents the beginning of Pagitt's sermon preparation. I asked Doug why he begins his sermon preparation this way and how long he has done so.

"We've been doing sermons this way pretty much from day one, and we do it like this for two reasons. First, it helps people see themselves as a part of this process. It makes the sermon a conversation, a communal thing, and not just my thing. Second, we get much better content this way. The sermon discussion we ultimately have on Sunday is way better when the thoughts come from the community and not just from me."[29]

We opened the May 5, 2009 Tuesday sermon discussion gathering by reading Acts 1 and 2 straight through and out loud. Each person in the circle read a chunk and then handed off to the next person. Doug then asked what grabbed us or jumped out at us, and from there we were off and running.

> *"Is this Holy Spirit that is poured out in Acts 2 different from the Spirit of God that is around in the Old Testament and hovering over the waters at the time of creation?"*

> *"I'm amazed at Peter's growth in these couple chapters. Even in Acts 1:6 he's still sort of asking the wrong question. But the speech he gives in 2:14–36 is totally amazing, quoting Joel, tying in Psalm16. He nails it here!"*

> *"Why does Jesus have to leave for this Holy Spirit to come?"*

> *"The Jewish celebration of Pentecost commemorates the giving of the Law to Moses fifty days after Passover, right? So is the Christian celebration tied to that in any way?"*

29. Pagitt, interview.

"*I grew up in a Pentecostal tradition where speaking in tongues was a big emphasis. It was sort of the gateway gift of the Spirit, like until you got glossolalia you weren't going to receive or experience any of the other gifts. How much does the biblical Pentecost really have to do with all that?*"

"*Isn't this whole Pentecost event about leveling the playing field and doing away with both the hierarchy of leadership and the exclusivity of Christianity? All the different languages seem to open the gospel to people of all cultures and lands. And the Holy Spirit descends upon everyone, not just the twelve.*"[30]

I was astonished at the level of the discussion and the depth of insights shared. It was clear that these folks were more than just biblically literate. Not only were other passages in the Luke-Acts corpus brought into the conversation, but in the course of our ninety minutes together, we flipped to Genesis 1, Exodus 20, Numbers 11, I Samuel 19, and a half dozen other passages, all of which somehow illuminated and enlivened the first two chapters of Acts. I learned a ton from these folks and their lively discussion.

The hour and a half flew by. Doug closed the gathering by suggesting that, since their corporate look at Pentecost would last three Sundays, they begin this first Sunday with a discussion of the Jewish background and the Old Testament form of the celebration. This would enable the community to look at the wealth of Old Testament texts the sermon group had uncovered and provide some helpful background for the subsequent weeks.

I asked Doug what he does with the wealth of material after each Tuesday night discussion. His discipline from Wednesday to Sunday is "to try to incorporate and reflect something that each and every person said Tuesday into the Sunday sermon." I noted how difficult that might be given the wide-ranging nature of the discussion. "I've definitely freed myself of the need to put it all together into some unified whole. I actually want our collective discussion on Sunday of any particular text to stay spread out and remain as broad as possible."[31]

To those of us with more traditional approaches to preparing sermons—closing our office doors, reading various translations, commentaries, and typing away at our computers—Pagitt's communal approach to the sermon seems both risky and unpredictable. "You know, at the be-

30. Sermon Discussion Group, Solomon's Porch living room, 5 May, 2009.

31. Pagitt, interview.

ginning of all this ten years ago," Pagitt said, "I suppose I thought of this as a risky approach, letting everyone say something and weigh in. But now it feels extremely safe. It's not just my sermon or my thoughts; it's everyone's. There's tremendous comfort and strength in that. It's not just me out there every Sunday evening."[32]

As with so much that I experienced in my time at Solomon's Porch, I felt that all the sermon preparation participants, including Pagitt, were doing something more risky than they realized. The participants in the community had not just been included in, but empowered by this Tuesday evening study group. They have grown to be comfortable doing something millions of other lay people would never dare to do, sitting down with a well trained, highly educated, prolifically published pastor and offering their opinions and interpretations of a biblical text. Yet even this risk within the context of their years in the Solomon's Porch community has come to feel quite comfortable and ordinary. For at the Porch, these folks have been given opportunity after opportunity not only to find and use their own voices, but to shape and influence the message their community will hear on Sundays. And as for Pagitt, no matter how comfortable and safe he has come to feel with this communal approach to sermon preparation, he is still making himself vulnerable by opening his mind and heart to the insights of the group week in and week out. To his credit, Pagitt has masterfully woven this sermon preparation process into the fabric of life at the Porch, so that it doesn't feel like risk to anyone. That's the beauty and the transforming power of a risk taking community. As my friend and editor Dr. Randy Evans put it, "When you lose control, for the first time you feel in control; when you let go, you find out what is truly worth holding onto."[33]

I know that I would be a better disciple in a community like Solomon's Porch. I know that I would be up for the many invitations I would receive in the context of that risk-taking community. I know that my life would be closer to the abundant one Christ promised in John 10:10, and that I would be much more likely to invite others in my life, regardless of their faith stance or religious persuasion, to "come and see" what I was experiencing in the Solomon's Porch community.

32. Ibid.

33. Evans, Randy. Conversation with author. Harbor Springs, MI., 28 Sept. 2009.

Thanks to communities like Solomon's Porch, I am not afraid of the accelerating decline of the institutional Church. Instead, I look with enthusiasm to the exciting communities of practice that are emerging to take her place. I'm grateful to Solomon's Porch and to those other bold communities of practice for giving me a glimpse of what is possible when a community is willing to be vulnerable and to take Christlike risks together. I know that I never would have risked leaving my stable, comfortable, well-paying position and pension to start a new and very vulnerable community here in Northern Michigan without seeing, through other fledgling communities, that it actually could be done.

But even for those still laboring in the fields of traditional, denominational Christianity, there are plenty of applicable lessons from a risk-taking community of practice like Solomon's Porch. There are important questions that can and should be asked even in a more traditional faith community, such as how might we make the sermon a more communal endeavor and expression instead of just the pastor's thoughts? If the word "liturgy" originally meant "work of the people," how might we involve our communities in doing that work with integrity and creativity on a weekly basis? What would it look like to construct and operate under a budget that intentionally keeps us vulnerable and on the edge rather than securing our future? How might we get our churches to understand and embrace the fact that we're only to exist as long as we are finding ways to bless the world and those outside our community, that we were never meant to exist for ourselves?

Generally speaking, the educational programs traditional churches set up are designed to feed their own membership, to increase their members' knowledge of scripture or their understanding of their mission. But what if Christian Education also meant setting up opportunities for members of the community to take Christlike risks together outside of the church building? What if a congregation set up an investment club, where the participants invested their money in NGO's, non-profits, and other people centered services, where the aim wasn't one's own financial gain but rather to maximize the welfare of others? What if a church chose to become "homeless," to give up its building for some greater purpose and opted to become dependent on existing facilities in the community? What might that do to a congregation's understanding of itself and to its ability to engage in more significant mission?

At some point, any collection of Christ followers must ask a very basic question: Why, when Jesus sent the twelve out to teach, preach, and heal, did he say, "Take nothing for the journey—no staff. no bag, no bread, no money, no extra shirt."[34] Might it be that Jesus knew something of the value of living in risk and vulnerability, something that we, in our constant quest for security and sustainability, have missed?

I will close this chapter with the very same quotation with which I opened it:

> Each of us is born with two contradictory sets of instructions; a conservative tendency, made up of instincts for self-preservation, self-aggrandizement, and saving energy, and an expansive tendency made up of instincts for exploring, for enjoying novelty and risk— the curiosity that leads to creativity belongs to this set. We need both of these programs. But whereas the first tendency requires little encouragement or support from the outside to motivate behavior, the second can wilt if it is not cultivated. If too few opportunities for curiosity are available, if too many obstacles are placed in the way of risk and exploration, the motivation to engage in creative behavior is easily extinguished.[35]

May all of us who claim to follow Jesus be forever in the business of cultivating that second tendency in ourselves and in one another, the expansive tendency for exploring, for creativity, for curiosity, and for risk.

QUESTIONS FOR DISCUSSION

1. Reread the quotation with which Jones opens and closes Chapter 3. Has your community of faith been more nurturing of your "conservative tendency" or your "expansive tendency"? Give some concrete examples.

2. Have you or has anyone you know tried to practice Christianity without any connection to a congregation or faith community? Discuss the benefits and drawbacks of such an approach to discipleship.

3. Have you traditionally thought of the practice of your faith as "risky business"? What is your reaction to the biblical passages Jones cites as evidence of the dangerous nature of our faith? Are there other passages that should be considered in this discussion?

34. Luke 9:3, NIV.
35. Csikszentmihalyi, 70.

4. Debate the pros and cons of Brian McLaren's term "community of practice." How does it differ from the term "church" or "congregation"? Do you think it matters what we call our communities of faith? Why or why not?

5. Respond to Doug Pagitt's claim that "The biggest threat to any Christian community is its sustainability—the drive to see to it that it will exist forever . . . We should only be around as long as we're doing things that allow us to be a blessing to the world"

6. Pagitt also insists that all churches "have risk, humility, and vulnerability in their histories," but have "forgotten where they've been," and "lost touch with those chapters in their history." Does anyone in the group know any stories from the history of your congregation that reveal its vulnerable and risky times? If not, could you find some?

7. At one point in the chapter, Jones tells a story of a homosexual participant at Solomon's Porch essentially "coming out" to his community during the worship hour. Can you imagine such an occurrence in your faith community? Why or why not? Speculate as to what might happen if such an event did occur in your context.

8. What do you think of the way Doug Pagitt prepares his sermons? Would you and your pastor(s) be open to trying such an approach in your community of faith? Why or why not?

9. Throughout Chapter 3, Jones makes the point that a community is necessary for any of us to take Christlike risks consistently. Do you agree? Why or why not? Can you offer the group any specific examples to support your point of view?

10. Jones says that, "At some point, any collection of Christ followers must ask a very basic question: Why, when Jesus sent the twelve out to teach, preach, and heal, did he say, 'Take nothing for the journey—no staff. no bag, no bread, no money, no extra shirt.' Might it be that Jesus knew something of the value of living in risk and vulnerability, something that we, in our constant quest for security and sustainability, have missed?" Respond.

4

Radical Inclusiveness

A T THE HEART OF the life and death struggle in which the Church finds herself is the fundamental question of who and/or what constitutes a church? Is the Church a pure, holy, and chosen community that stands fortified against an evil and corrupting world? Or is the Church a body of imperfect, blemished disciples, struggling to discover and cooperate with the unfolding will of God as best she can?

In some ways, the tension in which today's Church finds herself is not much different than the battle Donatus and St. Augustine waged centuries and centuries ago. The Donatists were supporters of a North African bishop in the fourth century, who contended that the purity of the Church was its central identifying mark. Furthermore, for Donatus, the Church's all-important purity was completely dependent on the purity and character of her presiding bishops. If the bishops were in any way corrupt or compromised, or if any impure men were admitted to this office of leadership, the Church, according to the Donatists, would lose her purity and thus her identity. It follows, then, that Donatus and his followers were fiercely committed to protecting the purity of the church, no matter what the cost.

Though we might not hear the name of Bishop Donatus much anymore, his legacy and perspective continue to be at work in the Christian Church today. And, to be fair, Donatus didn't start all this. As far back as the first century A.D., Peter and Paul were doing battle over whether Gentiles should be included in the Gospel message, and the question of who is in and who is out has raged on ever since. In the nineteenth and twentieth centuries, virtually every major denomination wrestled with whether women were worthy enough for ordination. And today, my denomination—the Presbyterian Church USA—is poised to split and splinter itself over the question of whether gays and lesbians are worthy of ordination and leadership. We Christians are forever drawing lines around our Church in an attempt to keep ourselves in and certain other people out. Donatus would be thrilled to know that his exclusive tendencies are still thriving in the twenty-first century Church.

It was St. Augustine, the Bishop of Hippo, who most vehemently objected to the Donatists' perspective. Augustine's contention was that the church had never been pure and was never intended to be pure. Augustine pointed to the original twelve disciples as proof of Jesus' obvious lack of interest in a pure church. Augustine went on to write of the Church that, "The man who enters is bound to see drunkards, misers, tricksters, gamblers, adulterers, fornicators, people wearing amulets, assiduous clients of sorcerers, astrologists . . . He (one who enters the church) must be warned that the same crowds that press into churches on Christian festivals also fill theaters on pagan holidays."[1]

Wherever our understanding of "Church" is on the continuum between Donatus and Augustine, it is vitally important that we understand and accept that while these purity battles still garner a lot of press, it is a smaller and smaller remnant that still speaks on Donatus' behalf. The postmodern world has left Donatus in a theological dustbin. To our children and grandchildren, the notion of a church—or any human organization for that matter— claiming to have any purity to protect is both preposterous and laughable. To put it bluntly, while the aged elders and most conservative fringes of my denomination argue vehemently against homosexual ordination, the millions upon millions of those who will never darken the doors of our churches fail to see what all the fuss is about. They have already moved light years beyond such labeling and line drawing.

Let me be clear: I am not asking anyone to agree with post-modern perspectives, particularly with regard to the ordination of homosexuals. But if you are a part of a Christian church and you want that church to be anything other than a rapidly dying and irrelevant institution; if you have any hope of engaging younger generations in the Jesus of the scriptures, you're going to have to embrace a more Augustinian understanding of who and what constitutes the Church rather than a Donatist one. In short, you are going to have to accept that the church of Jesus Christ is, always has been, and always will be a hospital for sinners and not a hotel for

1. Augustine, de cat. rud. xxv, 48.

saints. And that means accepting the fact that we sinners already in the hospital practice gluttony, lust, the hoarding of wealth and possessions, adultery, and pornography use, all of which Jesus would put on equal footing with murder.[2] As Barbara Brown Taylor reminds us, "Human beings may separate things into as many piles as we wish—separating spirit from flesh, sacred from secular, church from world. But we should not be surprised when God does not recognize the distinctions we make between the two."[3] Jesus did not rank sin nor did he give us license to do so. That's what Matthew 5 is all about.

Though I am a life-long Presbyterian, I have never been a huge fan of John Calvin. But there is one aspect of his massive theological corpus that is re-emerging and, I believe, will become absolutely central in the resurrected communities of Jesus. I am speaking of his notion of the "invisible church."

For Calvin, the earth would always be populated by both a visible church—folks who connect with and identify themselves as a part of an official body of Christians—and an invisible church—those not connected with any particular church or Christian body but who are still children of God and participants in his will. Only God knows the membership of this invisible church, according to Calvin. From a scriptural standpoint, Jesus could have been alluding to the invisible church when he told the scribes and Pharisees that sinners and tax collectors would enter the kingdom before religious leaders would.[4] One might also turn to Hebrews 13:2, where the writer urges that we "not forget to show hospitality to strangers, for by so doing some have shown hospitality to angels without knowing it." The famous sheep and goats parable from Matthew 25:31 and following can also be read as a classic invisible church text. Here the king separates the sheep from the goats. As the sheep are welcomed into their father's kingdom, they are surprised and have no idea why they are worthy of such an honor. Conversely, the goats, which are directed to a fiery place of punishment, are equally shocked that they *aren't* a part of the kingdom march. When the king explains the fate of each group, he ties it *not* to their membership or lack thereof in a visible Christian community, but rather to their *actions* toward the poor and the suffering in their

2. Matt 5:21–48, NIV.

3. Brown Taylor, *An Altar in the World*, 15.

4. Matt 21:31, NIV.

midst: "When I was hungry you fed me; when I was thirsty you gave me drink, etc."[5] Crucial to our understanding of this passage is that neither the sheep nor the goats performed—or failed to perform—any acts of compassion to Jesus himself, but instead to the "least of these" with whom Jesus so closely identified. We should also note, particularly in light of our previous discussions in Chapters 1 and 2, that no one in this passage is welcomed or congratulated for right belief, correct theology, or membership in the right religious society. It is concrete, compassionate action in the face of human suffering that counts.

The post-modern mind and heart cannot fathom, much less embrace, any god who accepts some and condemns others based solely on the cultural or religious group to which they belong. A huge cultural shift has occurred on this very point that makes the generation gaps of previous ages seem miniscule by comparison. Part of it has to do with the fact that America's younger generations have grown up not only in close proximity to, but in regular interaction and relationship with people of all races, nationalities, religions, and sexual orientations. American pluralism is a fact of life that is here to stay. As one friend of mine put it, "My son's PhD advisor is a Muslim. His roommate is a Jew. His students in the graduate seminars he teaches come from a dozen different countries. His apartment is adjacent to a B'hai Temple. He's dating an African American woman. And the most amazing part of all this to me is that he doesn't think twice about any of it." It's in light of such realities that John Shelby Spong asks rhetorically, "Can Christianity in particular, or any religious system in general, continue to define any human being as subhuman or second class by nature and expect to be taken seriously by anyone?"[6]

So we Christians shouldn't be at all surprised when the first question posed to us by those who are outside the church is, "How can you claim that your religion or version of faith is better or more true than any other?" The question in more evangelical terms is often phrased like this: "How can Jesus be the only way?" Any religion or faith group which claims a monopoly on religious truth or salvation these days will be hard pressed to attract, much less engage, the post-modern generations in their congregation. Without a respectful understanding of Calvin's invisible church and a genuine acceptance of the possibility of more than one way to God, Christianity will only accelerate its own demise.

5. Matt 25:35–36, NIV.

6. Spong, *The Sins of Scripture*, 78.

Having written what I have so far in this chapter, I can already feel the charges of heresy and universalism oozing toward me through these pages. But follow this part of my argument through to its conclusion. When I read and seek to faithfully interpret the scriptures, I look at any part of them in light of the whole. That whole for me has a trajectory, a movement, and an undeniable direction. I would characterize that movement as going from a narrow, very exclusive tribalism to an ever-widening inclusion. What began as a tiny covenant between Abraham and God, moved outward through the split branches of Jacob and Esau, out through the Sinai to Egypt, Moses, and the Israelites, and onto what we think of as the many branches of Judaism. Once Jesus entered the fray, the circle of God's love and mercy widened still further to include Samaritans, Gentiles, and finally, in the Great Commission of Matthew's Gospel, "all nations."[7]

Admittedly, this trajectory has been anything but smooth and un-contested as it fanned out. The Hebrew Scriptures reveal several key moments in Israel's history when the covenant people concluded that their problems—exiles, lack of peace, and loss of prosperity—had resulted precisely from *too much* inclusion, intermarriage, and accommodation to the surrounding cultures. So at several key points in Israel's history— such as when they prepared to cross over the Jordan with Joshua or when Ezra and Nehemiah returned from Exile to rebuild the temple and the walls of Jerusalem—Israel's leaders contended that God's will was for His people to remain pure, holy, and set apart from all other nations and peoples.

These interruptions in the expansive trajectory of God's love reflect the human desire to retract into exclusivity—what Csikszenthmihalyi called our "conservative tendency"—rather than embrace a change in God's plan.[8] Such retreats into exclusive conclaves are found in the Christian scriptures as well as the Hebrew texts, particularly in John's gospel and epistles. Paul also battled with his own exclusivist leanings at several points in his letters, as did the author of Hebrews.

But nonetheless, despite these periodic Donatist blips in the radar, the ever-widening, all-inclusive nature of God's love carried the day, as this monotheistic faith of ours moved forward through history. Acts

---

7. Matt 28:19, NIV.

8. Csikszenthmihalyi, *Creativity: Flow and the Psychology of Discovery and Invention*, quoted in Doug Pagitt and Tony Jones, An Emergent Manifesto of Hope (Grand Rapids: Baker Books, 2007) 70.

10:1–48, Galatians 3:28, John 10:16 are other key spots where the larger Divine impulse of inclusiveness reestablishes itself.

In some recent exegetical work I did for a sermon series on Jesus' healing miracles, I discovered, quite by accident, further proof of this clear biblical trajectory toward radical inclusion. Before turning to the gospels' healing stories, I read the entire book of Leviticus, Israel's law book, written specifically for her Levitical priests. This "Holiness Code" sought to keep Israel—and especially her priests—pure, holy, and set apart. (Leviticus must have been Donatus' favorite book in all of scripture!) The line that is most often repeated throughout Leviticus is: "You shall be holy, for I am holy, saith the Lord." Its chapter headings include such riveting topics as "Regulations about infectious skin diseases," "Discharges that cause uncleanliness," and, my personal favorite, "Rules regarding mildew." But what occurred to me as I studied this Old Testament law book was that virtually every healing situation Jesus encountered was one that had been clearly and specifically forbidden by Levitical laws. And yet, in every single case, Jesus knowingly, willingly, and blatantly violated the laws of purity and holiness set forth in Leviticus when he healed someone in the gospels. So Jesus' healings weren't simply miracles or demonstrations of his power; they were acts of protest. They were all about protesting the Jewish infatuation with laws of purity, an infatuation that would seep into Christian theology centuries later.

Below, I have paired excerpts from the Levitical code with a particular healing story that depicts Jesus acting in direct violation of the Holiness Code to clarify this crucial point that he is no Donatist.

> "When anyone has a rash or a bright spot that becomes an infectious skin disease . . . he shall be pronounced unclean . . . He must wear torn clothes, let his hair be unkempt, cover the lower part of his face, and cry out, 'Unclean! Unclean!' He must live alone, outside the camp."[9]

In Luke 5, Jesus encounters one leper, and in Luke 17 he encounters ten more. These interactions clearly fall in the Leviticus category of 'infectious skin disease,' and yet Jesus not only lets these lepers approach him, but he reaches out and touches them as well.[10]

9. Lev 13:2–3, 45–46, NIV.

10. Luke 5:12–14, 17:11–19, NIV.

"For the generations to come, none of your descendants who has a defect may come near to make an offering to God. No man who has any defect may come near; no man who is blind or lame, disfigured or deformed, no man with a crippled foot or hand . . . may go near the curtain nor the altar for he will desecrate my sanctuary."[11]

With this particular law, we could think of any number of healing stories, for Jesus healed many blind, lame, and physically deformed people in all four gospels. But the man with the withered hand whom Jesus heals in the temple on the Sabbath in Mark 3 comes most readily to mind. "Then Jesus asked them, 'Which is lawful on the Sabbath; to do good or to do evil, to save life or to kill?' But they remained silent. He looked around at them in anger and, deeply distressed at their stubborn hearts, said to the man, 'Stretch out your hand.' He stretched out his hand and was completely restored. Then the Pharisees went out and began to plot with the Herodians how they might kill Jesus."[12]

"When a woman has her regular flow of blood, her impurity will last seven days and anyone who touches her will be unclean...Anything she lies on or sits on will be unclean . . . Whoever touches her bed or anything she sits on will be unclean . . . And when a woman has a discharge of blood for many days at a time other than her monthly period . . . she will be unclean as long as she has the discharge."[13]

This story, of course, points us to the bleeding woman in Luke chapter 8, who has been suffering from some sort of bleeding or hemorrhaging for years! This poor woman epitomized uncleanliness and couldn't go anywhere, according to Leviticus' Holiness Code. But she defiantly goes out in public to a very crowded place, trying to get to Jesus, and pushes her way through the crowd, rendering every person she brushes up against unclean. Finally, she touches Jesus, making him unclean as well. And what does Jesus do? "Jesus says, 'Someone touched me. I know that power has gone out from me.' Then the woman, seeing that she could not go unnoticed, came trembling and fell at his feet. In the presence of all the people, she told why she had touched him and how

11. Lev 21:16–23, NIV.
12. Mark 3:4–6, NIV.
13. Lev 15:25, NIV.

she had been instantly healed. Then he said to her, 'Daughter, your faith has healed you. Go in peace.'" Notice that Jesus ends up blessing her! He praises her for her faith and, implicitly, for her defiance of the Levitican Holiness Code.[14]

Last but not least,

> "When any man has a bodily discharge, it will make him unclean . . . Whoever touches the man who has the discharge . . . will be unclean . . . Whoever sits on anything that the man with the discharge sat on will be unclean . . . His bed will be unclean and anyone who touches his bed will be unclean."[15]

Jesus' violation of this component of the Holiness Code is perhaps his most blatant violation of all. It occurs in the Good Samaritan parable in Luke 10. Here Jesus blows the whole Levitican Holiness Code completely out of the water! Think of it: the man who has been beaten and is on the roadside bleeding is emitting a bodily discharge. Therefore, he's unclean. This is precisely why the first two passers by—both priests—don't bother stopping to help this wounded stranger. But the third man, the Good Samaritan, not only stops, he touches the man, making himself unclean. To make matters worse, the Samaritan then puts the bleeding man on his donkey, making his donkey and everyone who subsequently touches or sits on that donkey unclean. The Samaritan then takes the injured man to the inn, where he gets him a bed—making the bed unclean—and the innkeeper, who will soon touch and wash those linens, will, of course, be rendered unclean as well.

In this, Jesus' most famous parable, he thumbs his nose at Israel's Holiness Code. He's telling the people of Israel, and especially their priests, that God is not nearly as interested in our purity as He is in our compassion, compassion directed to those who are suffering, those who are alone, those who are forgotten, passed by, or unclean.

When we examine Jesus' healing actions in light of the Levitican Holiness Code, we can't help but recognize that Jesus intentionally defied

---

14. Luke 8:42–48, NIV.

15. Lev 15:5–7, NIV.

these laws in both his actions and in his teachings. And Jesus' anti-Leviticus actions go way beyond just the healing stories. Remember the prostitute who barged in on one of Jesus' dinner parties and started anointing him with oil? This woman couldn't have been more unclean, and yet Jesus welcomed her touch, despite all of the Pharisees' objections. What about the Prodigal son? That younger son who went off on his hedonistic journey made himself as unclean as any Jew possibly could! He not only frequented brothels, he even took a job feeding pigs, where he both ate with and lived with pigs! Talk about unclean, unkosher, unworthy! Jesus' prodigal son was the poster boy for Levitican unclean-ness. And yet what does Jesus have the prodigal's father do in the story? He runs to the prodigal and throws his arms around this completely defiled boy. Why . . . because his compassion got the best of him. The father's compassion won out, which is exactly what Jesus wants from *all* of us yesterday, today, and tomorrow.

What I discovered, both in this study of the healing stories and beyond, is that Jesus conducted a direct, frontal assault on Israel's Holiness Code, as it had been expressed in Leviticus. I'd always known that Jesus took issue with some of Israel's laws, but I never fully realized that Jesus was on such a systematic campaign to dismantle Israel's infatuation with being "holy," "set apart," and somehow purer than the rest of the world. For centuries, the Jews had been convinced that the only way to please God was to separate and remove themselves from whatever was dirty, common, undesirable, or sinful. Jesus came to set *them* and to set *us* straight.

The God we worship is no Donatist. God was and is far more concerned about our being compassionate to the commoner, the sinner, and the outcast than She is about our being pure. Jesus felt for the people who were being kept out of the temple because of their supposed uncleanliness. Jesus knew that the Godhead didn't look at someone who was blind, lame, or suffering from leprosy as less worthy, less lovable, or less welcome in the temple. And so, at every turn in his ministry, Jesus made it clear that it *isn't* purity and holiness that God wants from us; it's compassion. It's our inclusive acceptance of everyone—especially those judged as unclean.

What remnants of the Levitican Holiness Code are we still clinging to? Who are the people today that we consider a threat to the Church's purity or to our own? Who are we trying to keep out of our temples, our schools, or our communion celebrations? Who are the lepers of today?

If one looks at our churches, our denominations, and all our endless internal conflicts, s/he can't help but notice that Christians everywhere are still fighting over issues of purity—who's in and who's out, who's welcome and who isn't, who can administer and receive the sacraments and who can't. Yet Jesus couldn't have been any clearer on these matters. He took on the purity protectors with every friend he made, every disciple he called, every person he healed, every dinner party he threw, every story he told, and every new commandment he uttered. If we're still worrying about protecting the purity of our church, of our community, or of any of our practices, we have totally missed Jesus' point.

I believe that in Jesus, God was and still is asking Her Church to trade in our lingering purity concerns for compassion. God wants us to trade in our tendencies to exclude someone from full participation in His church. God wants us to trade in our Donatist desires that would have us withhold from others the free, unconditional grace of God. In exchange God will give us a Christlike heart that aches and bleeds compassion for everyone, no matter how sinful, how unclean, or how offensive to our sensibilities they might be.

Scripturally speaking, faith in Jesus is clearly not about protecting purity and holiness or setting ourselves apart from others; it is about moving beyond our tribal, national, ecclesial, or denominational boundaries and pouring out compassion indiscriminately, just as Jesus did.

Once again, whether you happen to agree with me or not, the more important question to consider is whether my argument makes sense to the post-modern mind, to those younger generations who have, by and large, left the Church. I would hope that as the long since de-flowered bride of Christ limps deeper into the twenty-first century, she would at least open herself to the biblical trajectory's truth—if not to the contemporary culture's truth—that radical inclusion is what the Lord requires of us.

We would be a lot better off if we adopted Barbara Brown Taylor's humility in these matters. "I am not in charge of this House (of God), and never will be. I have no say about who is in and who is out. I do not make the rules. Like Job, I was nowhere when God laid the foundations of the earth."[16] If we, in our institutional churches, continue in our arrogant, narrow-minded judgmentalism, we are hastening our "suicidal irrelevance" in the eyes of the millions we so desperately need among us if we are to have any sort of future at all.[17]

---

16. Brown Taylor, *An Altar in the World*, 13.

17. Spong, *The Sins of Scripture*, 109.

Talking or writing about radical inclusiveness is a lot easier than living it. Constructing a coherent Biblical rationale for unconditional love and acceptance has been infinitely easier for me than finding a Christian community which truly practices it. But I did find one such community in San Francisco, California. The Glide Memorial United Methodist Church is, far and away, the most open, accepting, and inclusive Christian community I have ever encountered.

On Sunday, April 26 at 10:20 in the morning, I arrived at the corner of Ellis and Taylor in San Francisco's Tenderloin district for the first time in my life. I saw the faded yellow building on the corner, bearing the sign for Glide Memorial United Methodist Church. I also saw a line beginning on the Taylor side of the building that ran half way up the block toward O'Farrell. Was it the line for the meals Glide serves to the homeless three times a day? Was it folks waiting for the next recovery group meeting?

As I approached the queue, I was struck by its diversity: people from many races, ethnicities, sexual orientations, genders, shapes, sizes, and ages. Not wanting to betray my ignorance, I took my place in line, figuring that if I kept my eyes and ears open, all would be clear soon enough.

People kept joining the line, greeting one another like old friends and introducing those whom they'd brought to the regulars. Most often it was hearty hugs that were exchanged, not the safer, more distant handshakes that I've come to expect at church. The tall, twenty-something man behind me shouted out to a passing friend, who was heading for the end of the line that now extended around the corner of Taylor and O'Farell. "Dude! You comin' to get some Glide?" "Oh yeah!" the friend responded. "I'm ready to dance, Ray, mon!"

A group of six or seven gay men just ahead of me in the line were in an animated conversation about the "Glide Ensemble" and what they'd heard about how to join it. It was then that I realized what I was in line for. It was the 11 a.m. Sunday worship service, what Glide called its "Celebration." I was in a line snaking around an entire city block, a half an hour ahead of time, to get into a church service! The line looked like the United Nations but felt more like the crowd waiting to get into a U2 concert. In an age when churches were emptying and struggling to stay afloat, here was one that had hundreds and hundreds of people lining up an hour ahead of time just to get in. I had four days to figure out how Glide had pulled this miracle off.

My detective work began in the Glide archives under the helpful guidance of Marilyn Kincaid. There I would discover that Glide's road to such unparalleled diversity and inclusiveness had been anything but smooth. While the church had been in this location since 1929, it really wasn't until Rev. Cecil Williams arrived in 1964, first to head up The Glide Urban Center and then to continue the incredibly forward thinking work of Rev. John V. Moore, that the seeds for such radical inclusiveness and unconditional acceptance were sown.

In the early 60s, Williams inherited a congregation of about thirty-five white folks, whom he described as "so ingrained and so hard-nosed about what they thought the church was and needed to be doing. But," Williams explained, "it was none of the stuff that was really significant, and so we began to really change this place."[18] And change it they did. Here are just a few highlights from the Glide archives, chronicling some of Rev. Williams' earliest actions:

Aug. 1964: Rev. Williams provides leadership in creating The Council on Religion and Homosexuality, a pioneer organization in the Lesbian/gay movement in the city of S.F., with offices at Glide.

Sept. 1964: Glide collaborates . . . to create a half-way house helping mentally disturbed persons re-enter the community.

Jan. 1965: Rev. Williams, chair of Committee Against Segregated Education, threatens boycott of S.F. schools in protest of de facto segregation.

Jan. 1965: Rev. Williams, along with six other ministers, challenges the SFPD for breaking up a private benefit for homosexuals sponsored by The Council on Religion and Homosexuality.

Aug. 1965: Rev. Williams leads civil rights picketers in protesting S.F. School Board's refusal to release racial headcount of city schools. The Superintendent concedes, asking school board to publish a census.

Aug. 1965: Rev. Williams forms Citizens Alert, a citizens group to investigate charges of police brutality.

18. Cecil Williams, interview by author, tape recording, San Francisco, CA., 29 April, 2009.

Jan. 1967: Rev. Williams provides assistance to link professional people with the indigenous poor and the establishment of a free medical clinic in the heart of the City's Fillmore district.

Feb. 1967: Article appears in S.F. paper criticizing the Glide Foundation for using the Lizzie Glide Endowment to fund social work and activism with homosexuals, drug addicts, and male prostitutes.

Mar. 1967: Glide sponsors a retreat for clergy and homosexuals, a dance for male prostitutes, and pays $1000 to Negro gang leaders as "peace monitors" to help quell a race riot.

Apr. 1967: Rev. Williams speaks at anti-Vietnam war protest, which begins at the Civic Center and ends with a march to rally at Kezar Stadium.

June. 1967: Glide hosts a protest of the City's official rejection of the deluge of hippie visitors during the summer. The Sunday celebration service featured S.F.'s controversial poetess Lenore Kandel, whose book was held as obscene in a trial.[19]

Clearly, the young Rev. Williams did not receive the same advice that I did upon entering the ministry, or if he did, he didn't follow it. That advice was "Don't make any changes or cause any waves in the first few years at any church." But these samples from 1964–1967 were a mere prelude to what was perhaps Rev. Williams' most controversial act of all, one which he described in riveting detail in his autobiography, *I'm Alive.*

> "A huge cross is fastened to the sterile white wall of the Glide Church sanctuary . . . It's burial time . . . They all know what I'm about to do, and all week long they've come to me . . . warned, pleaded, threatened, and argued . . . The cross had always been there . . . They simply couldn't live without it . . . They accused me of arrogance and blasphemy . . . They may have been right. Something was being killed . . . But it was a symbol of death that was dying . . . Did I have the power to take down the cross? . . . The head of a hammer plummets toward the chisel handle and meets it with a muted crack. The blade forges deeper into the widening gap behind the cross . . . As pieces of the cross are pried free, patches of wall are revealed . . . Chunk by chunk, the cross comes down, and

19. Social Action/Social Justice, Archives, Glide Memorial United Methodist Church, San Francisco, CA.

every time the workers pull a piece free they rip away a part of me.
The job is nearly done . . . "[20]

Within a few short years of arriving at Glide, Rev. Cecil B. Williams chose to remove from the front wall of the sanctuary the central, defining symbol—not only of Glide Memorial United Methodist Church—but of all Christianity. For any of us in parish ministry, it is an almost unfathomable act. And yet for Rev. Williams, it was totally consistent with both his theology and his ecclesiology. The cross was and is a symbol of death to many church outsiders. Some contemporary theologians have even called the cross a symbol of "divine child abuse."[21]

David Richmond, Glide's Director of Special Projects, reflected on Williams' removal of the sacred symbol. "I think Cecil felt that the people of this community were suffering enough. They didn't need another reminder of suffering on Sunday morning. They needed and still need to celebrate and affirm life."[22]

For Williams, the cross was another one of the trappings of faith, rather than the substance of faith. "The church is not a building. Wherever we went and whatever we did, that was the church. But a lot of people did not understand that. They wanted this *place* to be the church and had wrapped their whole notion of 'church' up in the four walls."[23] Rev. Williams went on. "To convey the message that it was what we *did* out in the larger community that made us the church, we knew we had to get rid of a lot of things: hymnals, bulletins, ushers, the choir, and the robes. We had to get rid of creeds and old language and everything that people had mistakenly come to rely on as church. Church is in the doing; it's not in the talking. It's in making sure that everyone is included and no one is left out."[24] The Rev. added with a sly grin, "And we didn't stop to talk about doing any of this. We didn't hold meetings on change. We just changed. We just did it." [25]

I was beginning to understand that Glide's multi-ethnic, multi-racial, multi-generational, multi-sexual orientation-ed community did

20. Williams, *I'm Alive*, 75

21. Carson, *Becoming Conversant With The Emerging Church*, 166.

22. David Richmond, interview by author, tape recording, San Francisco, CA., April 27, 2009.

23. Williams, interview.

24. Ibid.

25. Ibid.

not result from their congregation just being welcoming and friendly on Sunday mornings. Creating the truly diverse, radically inclusive community that Glide is today was an extremely difficult, comprehensive enterprise. It required bold leadership and a willingness to confront those fellow Christians who sought to protect tradition and their narrow understanding of "church." More than that, though, it also required Williams and his fellow leaders to place themselves in the very heart of the larger community's most thorny issues and concerns, a place most pastors wouldn't touch with a ten-mile pole.

But Rev. Williams has never had any illusions about the opposition his approach to ministry and to Glide would bring. "When you make a choice to really be the church, there will be trouble. And immediately there was trouble around here."[26] But neither Williams nor his cohorts have ever flinched in the face of such opposition. "Key to our theology at Glide is that you've got to take risks. If you live in risk, then you can also live in love."[27] Cecil knew that for Glide to become the radically inclusive, open community that he and his fellow leaders envisioned, major risks would have to be taken again and again and again.

One of those key fellow leaders is Janice Mirikitani, who co-founded the Glide Foundation with Williams in 1965. She brings a wealth of wisdom, experience, and passion to the Glide leadership team, not to mention her former captivity in one of the internment camps. Myrikitani is San Francisco's Poet Laureate and one of its most honored and decorated citizens. Her role has been pivotal in helping the Glide community *be* the church by developing programs that make a real difference in people's lives. She began at Glide when she had "already declared God dead in my life, and Jesus truly didn't have meaning for me other than as fable."

Mirikitani reflected upon Glide's unusual community, which has reshaped and enlivened her faith.

> "The blessing and the challenge of a genuinely inclusive community is that it is always unpredictable. The Glide community is based on liberation and on a liberating God. But what confuses people about liberation is that you can't control it. Too many people want to control who they meet, how they meet, what they meet. But if you are truly and radically inclusive, you learn that you cannot control any of that. The challenges of the kind of community we've

26. Williams, interview
27. Ibid.

forged at Glide are obvious. We cannot control the outcome. We cannot live our lives comfortably. We cannot make assumptions. We have to be open. And we cannot and will not determine what this community should look like or how it should behave."[28]

Mirikitani, Glide's president and Rev. Williams' wife, has helped develop many of Glide's eighty-eight programs, all of which are aimed at meeting the expressed needs of the 'least of these.' "All our programs started with people from the streets coming to us with a need," Mirikitani said.[29] "We had homeless women who needed mammograms, so we asked the Red Cross to send us their mobile mammography truck once a week. We raised the $40 per person to enable folks to get these vital tests. That led to getting Planned Parenthood involved, which led to networking with area services for battered women, and now we have this huge, comprehensive medical center."[30]

I noted that for these street people to feel comfortable and confident in coming to Glide, they must have had a lot of positive, fruitful interactions with Glide out in the streets of the Tenderloin over the years. Glide has no shortage of street credibility. Cecil chimed in. "It was the same with our recovery circles."[31] Janice nodded, adding, "We had African American men coming to Cecil, crying out for help with this Crack Cocaine. 'It's killing us! We can't stop. You've got to help us!'"[32] In dialogue with these desperate users, Glide's dynamic duo conceived of an innovative approach called "Recovery Circle," and turned to one of their own recovering parishioners, Janean Sylvia Reed, to run it.

"Glide had always been a refuge for me," Reed remarked. "As a victim of a lot of sexual abuse, I came to Glide not trusting anybody. But this was the first place I didn't feel everybody's eyes on me. Rev. Cecil Williams encouraged me to find my own voice, my own set of values, my authentic self. And Janice Mirikitani was the first real female role model I had of a strong, hard-working woman leading in an equal way with men. They

---

28. Janice Mirikitani, interview by author, tape recording, San Francisco, CA., April 29, 2009.

29. Mirikitani, interview.

30. Ibid.

31. Williams, interview

32. Mirikitani, interview

believed in me and fully trusted me with this, and that enabled me to trust in and believe in myself." [33]

Ms. Reed didn't have a lot to go on in developing these recovery circles from the ground up. "Cecil didn't have a lot of rules about how we were to run these programs. We could swear, get angry, and speak our truth. He trusted us entirely with this program. He'd sit in with us from time to time, always getting real and raw himself."[34]

I asked Reed if their recovery circles were based on the twelve steps of A.A. and she was quick to say, "No. I think Cecil saw early on that the twelve steps were created by and for middle class whites, who lived in a very different world from the Tenderloin. It was through working with our early circles and the first Crack Conference we hosted in 1989 that Cecil carved out our own way, which we call 'The Terms of Faith and Resistance.'"[35] Like so much of what Glide does, the Terms of Faith and Resistance begin by helping the addicts find and use their own voices and then empowering them to take responsibility for their own recovery.

I attended and participated in Glide's 11:00 a.m. recovery circle on April 28, 2009. Three individuals, all of whom had come through this very circle themselves and had been clean for years, facilitated the circle. The other six or seven participants were all over the spectrum of addiction and denial. It was a brutally honest bunch, who recognized half-truths and equivocations immediately and weren't afraid to call one another on their "shit." It was an extraordinary ninety minutes, gritty, raw, and real. It was utterly consistent with everything else Glide is and does. I would find out later that most everybody in the circle originally got connected to Glide through "the line," the thrice-daily food line for the homeless poor. Glide's volunteer feeding staff, many of whom were or still are homeless themselves, keep an eye out for any clients who are chronically doped up and get word to Janean Silvia Reed, who then connects with them and invites them to a recovery circle or to her office. Reed noted that she has seen and helped hundreds of addicts get clean and get their lives back through the various programs at Glide. "So many of them come back or call me and tell me about their lives, their families, their houses, their jobs. It's amazing. And I know what they're talking about because it happened

33. Janean Sylvia Reed, interview by author, tape recording, San Francisco, CA., 28 April, 2009.

34. Reed, interview.

35. Ibid.

to me too."[36] She choked back some tears, as she recalled her own journey from bondage to freedom. "Jan and Cecil have pure hearts. They see the good in everybody that comes around here. The utter acceptance you feel from the Glide community gives you a certain kind of trust to see yourself and find your own true self. That kind of trust allows you to be free. And once you break free, you're reborn and your life changes completely." She concluded, "I love the woman I've become here, my authentic self. There's a power here that has no boundaries."[37]

Glide's innovative recovery circles have become a national model emulated throughout the country. "Faith is in the doing," Cecil remarked. "What we're doing here only works if we show these people that we really care, that we want to help them find liberation, to find the power to choose."[38]

In 2008 alone, Glide provided nearly one million meals—free meals—to the homeless of San Francisco. These meals are served in the church basement three times a day, seven days a week, 365 days a year. Cecil noted that these meals "have to be in the building. I visited a church once in Dallas," Williams recalled, "that fed a lot of street people, but they put the food in bags and handed it to the hungry people outside their building, never inviting or allowing the people in." He paused, shaking his head sadly. "That's no way to lift people out of their isolation."[39]

I wondered if Glide's radically inclusive food ministry and her many recovery circles had anything to do with the make up of that line I stood in Sunday morning for worship. I thought of all the people I'd met at Glide in my week there who'd found their voice, been encouraged to speak out, and been welcomed back again and again, regardless of how many times they'd slipped up. Could that have something to do with demographics of that Sunday morning line for the Celebration service? I thought about the fact that in all the times I'd come and gone from Glide, from eight in the morning to eleven at night, there were always homeless people in the shadows and under the awning of that faded yellow building at the corner of Ellis and Taylor. They were safe there, free from bother. Maybe that's where some of that Sunday morning diversity came from? From

36. Reed, interview.

37. Ibid.

38. Williams, interview

39. Ibid.

where else could it come? From Glide's medical center that provides street people and uninsured folks with everything from HIV tests to mammograms to counseling? From Glide's after school programs for kids preschool through high school? From Glide's low cost apartments for people with dual diagnoses? From their recovery circles for all kinds of addicts? Could Glide's multi-everything complexion have resulted from her pastors and leaders being out in the jails, in the shelters, in the picket lines, and in the courtrooms, advocating for whomever was without power and without a voice?

I eventually arrived at the conclusion that Glide's genuinely open and radically inclusive community was forged intentionally and through constant risk taking. It was the result of their *being* the church out on the streets, in the neighborhoods, in the prisons, and in the shelters.

On my final evening at Glide, I attended their "Speak Out" session for the homeless. Every Wednesday evening from 5:00–6:00 pm, Glide opens their "Freedom Hall" to street people. There is a microphone at the front of the room, and anywhere from fifty to a hundred homeless folks come in and sit in rows of folding chairs. Right at 5:00, Rev. Williams and Janice Mirikitani walked in to the cheers of their homeless brothers and sisters. Cecil shuffled up to the podium and opened the session with the following call:

> "It's time! It's time; my time, your time, everybody's time. We all have voices, and when we use them we are powerful! We've all got something to say. We don't need anybody else to speak for us. We can speak for ourselves, and we're going to speak out tonight. If you can't say it here, I don't know where you can say it. Everybody here tonight is human. You might not always feel like it. You might not always be treated like it. But you are human. You've got something to say. So let's speak up and speak out."[40]

For the next sixty minutes, homeless men and women stood up one by one, walked proudly to that microphone, and spoke out. Some spoke in poems, some in song. Some told stories while others shared dreams. They were drug addicts, winos, and the mentally ill. They were black, white, Asian, and Latino. They were old, young, crippled, tired, bent over, and bounding with energy. They were in bondage to poverty and countless other demons, but they were liberated by that microphone and the

40. Williams, at the "Speak Out" gathering for the homeless in Glide's Freedom Hall, 29 April, 2009.

gathered community who was there with them, willing to hear whatever they had to say.

I, too, was empowered by their words. A voice rose up inside me. Four words, building in intensity. Four words, rising up, trying to speak out, to cry out: "This is the Church! This is the Church!"

Janice Mirikitani's remarks about liberation bear repeating.

> "The Glide community is based on liberation and on a liberating God. But what confuses people about liberation is that you can't control it. Too many people want to control who they meet, how they meet, what they meet. But if you are truly and radically inclusive, you learn that you cannot control any of that. The challenges of the kind of community we've forged at Glide are obvious. We cannot control the outcome. We cannot live our lives comfortably. We cannot make assumptions. We have to be open. And we cannot and will not determine what this community should look like or how it should behave."[41]

Glide Memorial United Methodist Church is a community of liberation. And just as Mirikitani says, they're not interested in controlling people or making their flock behave in a certain way. Not many of us are willing to give street people a microphone, a platform, and a genuine hearing. But if Glide is about anything, they are about helping everyone— everyone—find his/her voice. And when you commit to that, there are a whole lot of things that you cannot control. The model most dying churches have bought into, either consciously or otherwise, is to essentially silence the people. It is not the many voices the Church is interested in but the one voice, the voice of the pastor, the preacher, the trained and educated leader. This one voice approach is not only true at the vast majority of churches during their worship times each week, but also during their education programs and countless other ministries as well. But at Glide a radical decision has been made—a decision for liberation. And liberation cannot be achieved when one person speaks and the rest are silent, when one person leads and the rest follow.

I found it extremely significant that the two acknowledged leaders of the Glide community were and always are present when the homeless gather to speak out. Both Janice Mirikitani and Cecil Williams were in the front row, listening respectfully as their people spoke out.

---

41. Mirikitani, interview.

David Richmond, Glide's Special Projects Coordinator, picked up on this theme as he remembered adjusting to Glide in the early years of his twenty-five-year tenure there.

> Street people would come in for Celebration on Sunday mornings. Some would be stoned and others drunk. And every now and then one of these cats would just stand up and start yelling or saying something right in the middle of Cecil's sermon. And Cecil didn't mind at all. In fact, he engaged them! Not only did he not shush them, but he didn't let anyone else shut them down either. Cecil made it very clear to me and to everyone there that street people and dope fiends are every bit as much a part of the church as any of the rest of us.[42]

Rev. Williams mused that in a lot of ways being a part of Glide is like being a jazz musician. "There's a lot of improvisation going on here. If you know our melody, you can join in and improvise in your own voice. If you know what it means here to be the church, you can add your voice and your style to it."[43] Jazz is, indeed, an apt metaphor for the beautiful yet chaotic flow that is Glide Church. My sojourn there was intended to expose me to several parts, programs, and people within Glide. But the longer I was there, the more I realized that all these parts were not separate at all, but flowed freely and organically back and forth, into and out of one another. Many of the people I met first came to Glide through the food line. Many flowed from there into the volunteer staff, feeding and serving others. At some point they heard about the Celebration service and perhaps joined the Glide ensemble. Others first hooked up with Glide in the jailhouse, where they were referred to a caseworker or rehab counselor from Glide. That initial relationship flowed into one of Glide's recovery circles, which readied them for the work place. When a transitional place to live was needed, they might have flowed into one of Glide's hundreds of low cost units connected to or down the block from the church. One estimate had as many as thirty of Glide's current 120 employees originally coming from the streets, from the food line.

As thousands upon thousands of churches close their doors and cease to exist because they can no longer fill the pews and pay their heating bills, Glide will keep right on flowing. They have no doors to close.

---

42. David Richmond, interview by author, tape recording, San Francisco, CA., 27 April, 2009.

43. Williams, interview

They have decided that unconditional love means exactly that. There are no ifs, ands, or buts when it comes to whom Glide will love, accept, serve, and welcome. The rest of us in the institutional Church talk a lot about unconditional love and grace, but we are quick to draw boundaries around to whom we'll extend it. For many of us, "unconditional love" is for everyone as long as they aren't gay or lesbian. For others of us, "unconditional love" is for anyone who is willing to accept Jesus as Lord and Savior. For still others, "unconditional love" is for those who haven't had abortions or have not committed a serious crime. We in the institutional church are quick to say, with an air of humility, "we're all sinners." But what we really mean is "While none of us is perfect, your particular imperfections are ones we simply will not tolerate here." Glide Memorial United Methodist Church may be the only Christian church I have ever witnessed that truly places no conditions on who can be a part of their community and its ministries. At Glide the word "unconditional" actually means unconditional.

I once heard a preacher ask, "If your church closed its doors and went out of business tomorrow, who would protest? Would it be only a handful of your own 'members'?" He went on to assert that if a church was genuinely living the Way of Jesus and closed, there would be thousands upon thousands of protestors, namely the poor, the homeless, the hungry, the rejected, the despised, the widowed, and the addicted. Having finally experienced a radically inclusive, utterly diverse community at Glide, I can finally envision just such a protest.

But we can't all live and serve in San Francisco. The community in which I live has one African American person and a handful of adopted Chinese kids. In the summer we pick up a few migrant pickers from Central America, but that's pretty much it as far as diversity goes. We say we're open to all and even had an open communion table at my former church. But what can we learn or implement from Glide's radical inclusiveness?

For starters, the dominant model of ministry in this country is still based on the notion that our center of being is our building, and thus our goal is to get people to come to us—to our building. We still think that a church is a place, a place we want people to come for worship and other programs. Emergent pastor Heather Kirk-Davidoff, the leader of the Kittamaquandi Community in Columbia Maryland, put it brilliantly when she said, "I've stopped wondering how to draw younger folks into my church and started focusing on how to draw my congregation out of its building and into relationship with the world outside its doors."[44] This is precisely the paradigm shift that the Glide community has made, and it's one that could undoubtedly energize and even revolutionize Christian communities in the twenty-first century. Even if our streets in Middle America look a little different than they do on the California coast, there is no reason we can't be the church out in our streets, down the road in our trailer park communities, or in our neighborhood schools. No matter how homogeneous or diverse the community in which we serve, radical inclusiveness is conveyed by the same means—getting out of the building and meeting local needs indiscriminately.

The community that I am in the process of founding has no building and never will. We have forsworn the real estate business forever and ever, amen. Part of our intention is to be everything we are and to do everything we do out in the world, so that we never confuse who we are and what we're here for with a particular place or building. But even the millions of Christian churches and communities that *do* reside in temples made by human hands *must* remember that they are *not* barricaded in those temples. They can figure out their own way of heeding Heather Kirk-Davidoff's advice to "start focusing on getting their congregations outside the building and into the world." Are there any public elementary schools in your community that *aren't* looking for volunteer readers and tutors to come in a couple days a week? Are there any local nursing homes and care facilities that *don't* have at least a few residents who get no visitors? Are there any public parks in your community that *aren't* in need of some cleaning and periodic supervision? Do any of our communities *not* have hard working single mothers who are too exhausted to cook a balanced meal for their kids? Does your county jail have any inmates who don't get any visitors? Are there any widows and widowers in your neighborhood who are being neglected or forgotten? These are the things Jesus calls us to do, and they can be done anywhere, except, of course, in our church buildings.

But even within our church buildings there are Glide-like things we can do. We can open our communion tables to everyone—not just people who profess what we do or who have 'joined us' in membership. We can be sure that things like our choirs, youth groups, knitting circles,

44. Kirk-Davidoff, "Meeting Jesus at the Bar," 35.

Bible studies, and mission trips are not only open to all but are genuine purveyors of Christlike hospitality. And even those activities tradition- ally thought of as taking place inside the church can be taken outside the church to meet, celebrate, and serve.

I will never forget what the pastor of my home church did in the early 1980s, when our excellent choir grew to more than 200 strong. He walked into rehearsal one night, thanked everyone for giving so much to make our choir truly amazing. He then said that he didn't think our congrega- tion should have this massive choir all to ourselves, singing only for our own members, particularly when there were struggling churches within ten miles of us who had no choir at all. He then proceeded to divide the choir into three groups, each of which would sing in our church one Sunday per month. On the Sundays when one's particular grouping *wasn't* singing at our church, that group would go downtown to an inner-city church with no choir and sing there, so that on two Sundays a month, that struggling church would have a strong choir to lead them in worship. And on the fourth Sunday of each month, all three choral groups would reconvene to sing in full force at our home church. What a risky decision for our pastor to make! Yet what an undeniable act of hospitality and grace! What a reflec- tion of the gospel. None of us have ever forgotten the experience.

Radical, Christlike inclusiveness is, in so many ways, the best form of evangelism. A spiritual community that opens and extends itself to *every- one* can't help but point to a Deity who does the same. We can't all be in San Francisco, and we can't all be Glide Memorials either. But we must remem- ber that even Glide was once a very traditional, denominational congrega- tion! Only through bold leadership and intentional, Christlike risk taking did Glide became the beacon of radical inclusiveness that it is today. So no matter where we are and no matter what the complexion of our community, we, too, can endeavor to become "communities of practice," making sure that everyone in and around our community knows that they are welcome 'here'—welcome always and without any conditions. [45] Can anyone dispute that this is what Jesus would have us do?

Future communities of disciples will be genuinely diverse communi- ties, not just because they want to be or because it's somehow politically correct to be, but because they are so immersed in the streets, so intentional in their advocacy for the poor, so open to and respectful of every human being, and so committed to the hard work of justice and liberation for all.

45. McLaren, 80.

It has been Glide's consistent work over the last forty-five years in the streets of San Francisco that created that stunningly diverse, inclusive, and welcoming line I was in on that Sunday morning in April of 2009. And I can't help but feel that standing there was a little like standing in the kingdom of God. My heart continued to sing, "This is the church! This is the church!" I can only hope and pray that my faith community and yours will develop the open theology, the genuine discipleship, the willingness to take risks, and the radical inclusiveness required to join in Glide's beautiful and jazzy tune.

QUESTIONS FOR DISCUSSION

1. Do you find yourself more drawn to Donatus' or Augustine's understanding of the Church? Why? Which understanding guides your community of faith?

2. Jones writes: "If you want your church to be anything other than a rapidly dying and irrelevant institution, you're going to have to embrace . . . that the church of Jesus Christ is . . . a hospital for sinners and not a hotel for saints. And that means accepting the fact that we sinners already in the hospital practice gluttony, lust, the hoarding of wealth and possessions, heterosexual adultery, and pornography use, all of which Jesus would put on equal footing with the supposed sin of a homosexual orientation and life style." Do you agree with Jones here? Why or why not?

3. How might Calvin's concept of an "invisible church" be relevant and challenging to those claiming to follow Christ today?

4. Have you ever been asked, "How can you claim that your religion or version of faith is better or more true than any other? . . . How can Jesus be the only way?" How have you responded? Wrestle with these crucial questions as a group.

5. Review the pairs of scripture Jones offers from Leviticus and the Gospels. Have you ever thought of Jesus' healing miracles and parables as protests against Israel's Holiness Code before? Is the argument compelling? Why does it even matter?

6. What are your impressions of Glide Memorial United Methodist Church in San Francisco? Are there parts of Glide's ministry that make you uncomfortable? Which and why? Do you think these aspects of their ministry would make Jesus uncomfortable? Why or why not?

7. Jones makes a distinction between symbols—what he calls the "trappings of faith"—and the substance of faith. Rev. Williams does the same thing when he gets rid of things like "hymnals, bulletins, ushers, the choir, and the robes . . . everything that people had mistakenly come to rely on as church." Are there any symbols or trappings that you and your faith community may be overemphasizing at the expense of more substantive matters?

8. Jones asserts that "the model most dying churches have bought into . . . is to essentially silence the people. It is not the many voices the Church is interested in but the one voice, the voice of the pastor, the preacher, the trained and educated leader . . . But at Glide a radical decision has been made—a decision for liberation. And liberation cannot be achieved when one person speaks and the rest are silent, when one person leads and the rest follow." What model does your community seem to operate out of? What are the pros and cons of that model? Might it limit who gets involved in your community?

9. Who is missing from your faith community? Might you be doing something to contribute to their absence?

5

Service. Period!

SERVICE TO OTHERS HAS become fashionable again. Volunteerism is up. Everybody and his mother have short-term mission trips on their schedules in the coming year. Some high school and college kids are even taking "alternative spring breaks," going to poor regions in the Caribbean or even in the continental United States to build orphanages or do relief work when they could be heading off to Daytona to witness or even star in the latest "Girls Gone Wild" video. Every time another hurricane hits, a tsunami of do-gooders loads up their vans and heads to the eye of the storm.

By any standard, this trend has to be seen as a good one, a welcome change from decades of America's self-absorption. People seem to be seeking significance in their lives rather than merely success, perhaps finally realizing that a truly rich life is not attainable when all one's energies are self-directed. Congregations across denominational lines are waking up to the fact that without significant service to others, their churches are nothing more than country clubs. Christ issued a clear call to his followers that they not exist for themselves but for others, and that begins with taking care of the poor in our midst. (See Matthew 25:31–44) It's no wonder so many churches are calling themselves "missional" and writing mission statements in an attempt to show that they are not the self-serving, internally focused country clubs they often appear to be.

In the July 29, 2008 *Christian Century*, editor John Buchanan shared a compelling story about a New York City church, The Church of the Holy Apostles. This once thriving, landmark church came upon hard financial times and dwindling membership in the early 1980's. At its membership and budgetary nadir, the Bishop who oversaw this church assigned a new priest to Holy Apostles with the express task of closing the church and conducting its funeral. Once this priest arrived and assessed the situation, he convinced the consistory that The Church of the Holy Apostles ought to go out doing "something Christlike." So they began offering a free lunch program. The program initially served 35 folks but soon was serving 900. When roof repairs and some fire damage resulted in the pews being temporarily removed from the worship space, the church members decided to keep them out of the sanctuary for good, in order to create more table space for the now five-day-a-week feeding ministry. At the time of Buchanan's *Christian Century* article (July 2008), some twenty years after that first free meal was served, the Church of the Holy Apostles was serving 1200 meals per day at an annual cost of 2.7 million dollars.

Buchanan sought the reason or spiritual motivation for such a small church taking on such a large and unending task and then sustaining it for so long. One of their staff members replied, "Because Jesus said to feed the hungry. There's no more to it than that . . . In all the intricacies of scriptural interpretation, that message—feed the hungry—could not be more clear." Buchanan summarizes the significance of Holy Apostles' transformation from worshiping community to mission outpost in the final two sentences of his piece. "Maybe the world would find churches more interesting and compelling if they showed something of the love of Jesus in their lives and practices. Maybe there is no more important and life-giving strategy for every church than finding something Christlike to do."[1]

The St. Charles Avenue Presbyterian Church in New Orleans and its pastor Don Frampton found something Christlike to do in their context, but not because of a budget crunch or dwindling membership. For them it was a Hurricane named Katrina that brought them the opportunity to do something Christlike in the city of New Orleans. Pastor Frampton noted in a sermon he delivered in Harbor Springs, Michigan on August 10, 2008 that, "These years (since Katrina) have been the best years in the life of our congregation, when all our efforts have gone into rebuilding other people's homes, churches, and lives."[2] Frampton noted that Katrina relief gave his congregation a clear, well-defined mission, something it had never had before. He said that St. Charles Avenue could never and will never go back to the church it was before Katrina. The congregation simply will not allow it.

1. Buchanan, John. "Something Christlike." *CC* (July 29, 2008), 3.

2. Don Frampton, sermon delivered at First Presbyterian Church Harbor Springs, (8 October, 2008).

There is something compelling about simple, direct service offered in the name and spirit of Christ. Solomon's Porch founder Doug Pagitt goes so far as to say, "Serving our neighbors looks less like a sophisticated social service program than like a guy lending out his lawn mower."[3] But whether congregations and individuals take a simple or more complex approach to our missional endeavors, many of us wonder whether such service to the least of these on its own is enough. There is a strong evangelical mindset in many of us that causes us to question whether our good deeds to the poor are sufficient on their own, or whether they need to be supplemented with some sort of preaching or verbal explanation that includes the spoken name of Jesus.

For several years in the late 1980's, I was the director of a grassroots organization that provided emergency shelter to the homeless of Lake County, Illinois. We turned church basements and fellowship halls across the county into shelters from mid-October through early May on a rotational basis. As Thanksgiving approached in 1989, we received a call from a non-denominational church offering to provide the entire Thanksgiving meal at one of our sites, from the turkey and stuffing right down to the pumpkin pie. We accepted this church's offer, contingent upon their running through our volunteer training protocol, which included a segment emphasizing our strict prohibition against any form of proselytizing. This prohibition was based both on common decency and on the fact that as an organization receiving government funding, we had to avoid any and all traces of religious behavior, symbols, and conversations. But we also believed that the true spirit of Christlike hospitality called us to welcome and serve our homeless guests without asking anything in return, including having them listen to some religious sales pitch. So there we were in Waukegan, Illinois Thanksgiving night, 1989, when this church group showed up in force with a feast fit for royalty. As fate would have it, right about the time our homeless guests were to arrive, I was called out into the parking lot, where a policeman needed to speak with me. This was very commonplace, since the local police were supportive partners in our effort to get folks off the cold streets. My parking lot conversation took about ten minutes, and when I got back into the dining area, I noticed that our guests were not clumped together at the dinner tables like they usually were. Instead, they appeared to have been intentionally split up

---

3. Pagitt, *Reimagining Spiritual Formation*, 150.

into little groups of three—one homeless guest with two of the people from the non-denominational church. The church folk had their bibles open and were going over the "path to salvation" with our guests *before* they would serve them dinner! I was irate and immediately got rid of the Bibles and their bearers in a fashion reminiscent of Jesus' cleansing of the temple.[4]

Reflecting on this debacle later, I realized that this evangelical group was clearly under the impression that their gifts of food and hospitality were somehow not enough, and that to *make* their act of generosity "Christian," they had to speak and verbally explain their understanding of what gets a person to heaven. If they failed to verbally link this meal with their faith in Christ, in their minds the meal they provided would have been meaningless. Bad theology strikes again, begetting ugly Christianity.[5]

On the other end of the theological spectrum, in 2003 I took a group of kids from my church to Portsmouth, Ohio on a one-week mission trip through Group Workcamps Foundation. For a full week, our kids joined forces with about 400 others to work on homes that had been damaged by Ohio River flooding. The fifty-some homes our group worked on were spread throughout Portsmouth, and over the course of the week, the people of the town took notice of us, wondering who we were, what we were doing there, and why we were doing all this work for free. One of the houses we worked on was next to an elderly gentleman's home, and that neighbor sat on his porch and watched our kids work for four hot, humid days, never once venturing off his porch nor saying a single word. On the fifth day, he came over to the home being worked on next to his and asked us a few questions: Where were we from? Why were we here? Who was paying us? When it became clear to him that we were just a bunch of high school kids and leaders who had chosen to spend a week of our summer vacation helping out the people of Portsmouth, he asked if we could baptize him. He was almost eighty years old! He had grown up in a church family but never warmed up to the faith he saw in his family and in that church. But he said, "If all these kids are choosing to do this kind of work because of the God they worship and serve, I'd like to be a part of a team like that." Because I was off-site with a group of kids at the time, the group found another ordained pastor among the group leaders and celebrated his baptism on our last day at camp.

4. John 2:13–19 NIV.
5. Jones. *The New Christians*, 103.

It wasn't any preaching or explanation of the four spiritual laws that touched this old man's heart. There weren't any words involved at all. There was only the power of no strings attached service. The raw witness of love in action did more to lead this man to Christ than words ever could.

To me, these two stories depict the past and the future of Christianity and its mission. In the past, far too many followers of Christ have not trusted the transforming power of serving the poor and have felt compelled to top it off somehow with words or a catchy evangelistic message. In the future, communities of Christ will, like those Group Workcamps kids, realize that love in action is all that is ever needed. After all, Jesus never asked us to be his attorneys, arguing or persuading people into following him. He called us to be witnesses. As my friend in Haiti, a Sister in the Order of St. Joseph, puts it, "Genuine Christlikeness is a communicable disease, something that is caught rather than taught . . . We Christians need to tread very lightly, waiting and seeing what we should *do* more than what we should say," and I think Sister Rose is right.[6]

The post-Katrina ministry of St. Charles Avenue Presbyterian Church operates out of an understanding much like Sister Rose's. In an interview I conducted with their pastor, Don Frampton (29 October 2008), Frampton described what transpired in the days immediately following Katrina's devastation.

> Our session was spread out all over the place because we had all evacuated. I was in Houston using the offices of a Presbyterian church there. The first thing I did was call our treasurer and our chair of stewardship. I told them that I believed we would have to suspend all our plans for mission for at least a year and put everything we had into the relief and rebuilding efforts in our city. They both agreed and we set up a conference call with the entire session (about forty-six people). No one questioned this idea, and from there it became a question of pulling together a small team that could lead us effectively. We knew what we wanted to do but needed the right people with the right gifts to help us execute it.[7]

The emerging St. Charles Avenue plan, still being executed today, was to partner with New Orleans' Habitat for Humanity, focus on one

6. Sister Rose Mary Fry, interview by author, tape recording, Cap Haitien, Haiti, January 21, 2009.

7. Don Frampton, interview by author, tape recording, New Orleans, LA., October, 29, 2008.

particular city block, and completely rebuild it. The church formed a small non-profit organization called RHINO —Rebuilding Hope in New Orleans—funded it with about $500,000, and got busy inviting volunteers from all over the country to spend a week or more with them rebuilding a street called Ferry Place.

A half million dollars is a lot of money for any congregation, no matter how affluent, to raise for the good of those outside the church with absolutely no strings attached. But that is precisely what St. Charles Avenue Presbyterian Church did and is continuing to do. I was fortunate enough to take small groups from my church in northern Michigan to serve RHINO on two separate occasions, and I was astonished at what this single New Orleans congregation has done. They are, quite literally, pouring themselves and their resources out as an offering to the flood victims in their city. And they're doing all this without asking anything in return and without verbally evangelizing the folks who will live in the houses they build. They are trusting in the power of their actions to be enough. They are trusting in what I call "Service. Period!"

Frampton shakes his head in amazement as he reflects on what this experience has meant to his church, to his people, to the city, and to himself. "There is no going back. Even if we wanted to return to the kind of church we were before Katrina, we couldn't do it and we wouldn't do it. None of us would want to. We have a mission. Even when the Katrina work is all through, we will find something else to give ourselves to. We understand now at a profound and personal level that serving others is why we exist. That is what makes us a church."[8]

Is service "why we exist" as an institutional Church? If so, do our budgets reflect that? Does where we—clergy and laity—put our time and energy reflect that reason to exist? It's an incredibly important question. To a huge and extremely vocal chunk of Christians, service to the least of these is *not* what we're here for; converting the least of these is what we're here for. Using the Great Commission of Matthew, Chapter 28:16 and what follows it, the Evangelicals among us have interpreted the call to "make disciples of all nations" to mean convincing everyone who doesn't believe exactly as we do to believe exactly as we do.

What I want to emphasize here is my firm conviction that in those Christian communities that will endure into the future, "Service. Period!"

---

8. Frampton, interview.

will be their practice. Service: Period! means serving others without strings attached and without piling any theology or message on top of the work we do with and for others. For once we start meeting the needs of others *in order to* preach to or try to convert them, our service loses its Christlikeness, its authenticity, and its legitimacy. As pastor and theologian Rob Bell puts it in one of his Nooma videos, "Love with an agenda isn't really love."[9]

People all over the world who have been subjected to Christian missionaries know what it's like to receive service or goods from someone who has an ulterior motive or agenda. Digging a well for a thirsty village *so that* we can then share the gospel message with the villagers is not something Jesus would ever have done. Inviting a hungry stranger into our home for a meal *so that* we can then share with him our understanding of the path to salvation is very different than feeding him because he is a child of God. Doug Pagitt, founding pastor of Solomon's Porch, puts it this way: "We should love God and our neighbors without having ulterior motives for either of them."[10]

We're not fooling anybody when we serve in order to manipulate. The extensive research in Gabe Lyons and David Kinnaman's *unchristian* makes clear the fact that only "one third of young outsiders to the church believe that Christians genuinely care about them . . . Rather than being genuinely interested in people for their friendship, we (Christians) often seem like spiritual headhunters."[11] And that is a charge that was never levied against Jesus of Nazareth. The post-modern world wants nothing to do with manipulative do-gooders. It is, instead, hungry for an authentic faith that gives itself away in service with no strings attached and no ulterior motives: Service. Period! For how do we know that simply feeding and providing drink to those in need *isn't* the gospel? In Matthew 25, the famous sheep and goat's passage, Jesus seemed to consider such acts of genuine compassion sufficient for salvation.

Previously, I mentioned a struggling congregation in New York City that chose to do something Christlike by using their building and its kitchen

9. Bell, "*Bullhorn,*" from the *Nooma series*, produced and directed by Flannel, (Grand Rapids: Zondervan, 2005).

10. Pagitt, *Reimagining Spiritual Formation*, 148.

11. Lyons, Kinnaman, *unchristian*, 68–69.

to feed New York's hungry and homeless since the late 1980s. In that quarter of a century, The Church of the Holy Apostles, on the corner of Twenty-eighth St. and Ninth Avenue in Chelsea, has fed over 6.4 million meals without ever turning anyone away and without ever seeking to preach, teach, or proselytize.[12] Each day of the workweek, somewhere between twelve and thirteen hundred lunches are served to street people and the chronically poor. It's important to note that these meals are not sack lunches handed out to the guests at arm's length, nor are they eaten down in the church basement. Each meal is home cooked in the church's kitchen, a process that begins each morning at 6:30 and then is enjoyed in the sanctuary of this beautiful, historic Episcopal church between 10:30 a.m. and 1:30 p.m. That's right—*in the sanctuary*—the very space in which this congregation worships!

Program Director and Associate Rector Liz Maxwell believes that the space in which the meal is served is vitally important to the overall enterprise. "This is our best space, not an annex or a basement. The guests feel that. They know that this is the best room in our house, the place where everyone is important, welcomed, and fed."[13] Maxwell went on to explain that using the sanctuary for the feeding ministry has had just as deep an impact on the congregation at Holy Apostles as it has on the guests. "The meals we serve on Monday through Friday become for us an extension of the meal we celebrate on Sunday in the very same space. In addition to the primary purpose of the Holy Apostles Soup Kitchen, feeding hungry people, hospitality is a very important secondary goal of this ministry. Meeting where we do requires our parish to share its most sacred space and make it welcoming to our lunch guests."[14] And it must feel pretty welcoming, given the number of guests who, when they no longer need the food Holy Apostles provides, choose to come back and join the volunteer crew or even the paid staff of the soup kitchen ministry. One such "graduate" goes by the name of J. R. "I remember coming here back in the 80s when I was on the streets. Back then the line to get in to the church went from Ninth Avenue all the way back to Eighth. This church was always here for me—for anyone—no matter what. I thank God for this church and these people who serve here.

---

12. Liz Maxwell, interview by author, tape recording, New York, NY., May 12, 2009.

13. Maxwell, interview.

14. Ibid.

I'm so grateful that now I can return and give back."[15] J. R. currently directs a transitional housing program in the Bronx called "Freedom U.S.A." He visits the line at Holy Apostles a couple days a week to encourage the folks, to hand out fliers, and to explain his program to any who will listen. "The Bible says we're to love and help our neighbors. It's basic. There's no clearer call than that," J. R. said.

There are so many benefits that such a clear and focused program of Service. Period! creates, even beyond the hungry mouths that are fed. "It creates community," according to Associate Rector Maxwell, "community for the guests, for the volunteers, for everyone who participates." The program currently has over 300 volunteers from all walks of life and from every conceivable religious background, including no religious background. One long time volunteer I spoke with named Bob happened to be Jewish.

"No one religion has a monopoly on service. Caring for people in need is something all religions share. I'm an observant Jew, and two of our precepts are to feed the hungry and to perform 'mitzvoth'—good deeds for others. Here I work with Christians and Muslims who are on the very same page when it comes to serving others. We're all a part of something much bigger."[16]

Gene, another volunteer, is recently retired and is a Christian. He has only been helping out with the Holy Apostles' Soup Kitchen for about a year. "I've met so many nice people here, both the other volunteers and the guests. We treat everyone here as a very important person."[17] Like so many volunteers, Gene first found out about this program by seeing the long line in front of the church every day and then asking someone what was going on. "It's been a real eye-opener for me. Our guests include all kinds of people, but mostly very good people. I admire them for their perseverance, their courage, and their refusal to give up," Gene said. He went on to tell me about a group of junior high kids from New York's IS-52. "We've got a group of eighth graders who come to volunteer with us about ten times a year, great kids who love doing this and we love having them here." After a reflective pause, Gene concluded, "What we all share here,

15. J. R., interview by author, tape recording, New York, NY., May 12, 2009.

16. Bob, interview by author, tape recording, New York, NY., May 12, 2009.

17. Gene, interview by author, tape recording, New York, NY., May 12, 2009.

all the volunteers, is one thing: the desire to serve. Just to serve."[18] I could almost hear the period after the word "serve."

I would be remiss if I were not to mention the size of this congregation that has served 6.4 million meals at a rate of about 1300 per day over the last twenty years. The Church of the Holy Apostles has about 150 members. I was flabbergasted when I learned this. How in the world could a community so small do something so huge? "The soup kitchen grew in such a way that surprised everyone," Liz Maxwell noted. "When this whole thing began, Holy Apostles was a small congregation without much going on. But right from the beginning the people here in the parish seemed to know just how important this was."[19] And together, the congregation kept rising to the growing challenges and opportunities feeding the hungry presented.

Fortunately, it wasn't only the people of Holy Apostles who understood the importance of their soup kitchen program. People throughout the city—individuals, congregations, and corporations—saw or heard about the rapidly growing line outside this small church and came forward to help in a variety of ways. Today, according to Mark Walter, the soup kitchen's Development Assistant and Webmaster, 50 percent of the soup kitchen's $2.6 million annual budget comes from individuals, 30 percent comes from foundations, and the remaining 20 percent comes from corporations, congregations, and the government. The soup kitchen operates at a cost of about $11,000 per day and has twenty-eight employed staff, half of which are full-time.[20]

Looking at where the 300 plus volunteers come from, only ten to fifteen—roughly 4 percent—come from The Church of the Holy Apostles itself. Sixteen percent of the soup kitchen's volunteers are Jewish, and the Roman Catholics outnumber the Episcopalians by quite a bit. A large percentage of volunteers have no religious connection at all.

The point of all these breakdowns is that when service is done in a no strings attached, no questions asked, "Service. Period!" sort of way, it transcends denominational and even religious divisions. The Holy Apostles Soup Kitchen, precisely because it operates out of a "Service. Period!" approach, has brought people together who, under any other cir-

18. Ibid.

19. Maxwell, interview.

20. Mark Walter, interview by author, tape recording, New York, NY., May 12, 2009.

cumstances, would never even have met, much less become friends and co-workers. That no strings attached approach has also enabled the soup kitchen to access funds for its feeding operation—including government funds—because all soup kitchen funds are kept separate from the church's general fund and from all other monies used for religious purposes. While the soup kitchen remains a crucial part of the church's mission, the Holy Apostles' Soup Kitchen maintains an entirely separate budget from the parish. In addition, an extremely diverse group of social service agencies has come forward to offer additional assistance to the folks who eat at Holy Apostles. Maxwell reports that, "We now have counseling services, HIV outreach, housing advocates, chiropractic care, and even a writers' workshop, all of which are available to our guests free of charge."[21] Would such an eclectic and vital mix of resources ever have come forward if Holy Apostles were in the conversion business, topping off each day's lunch with some preaching or a run-down of The Four Spiritual Laws?

Yet even without any sort of verbal evangelism, the soup kitchen has produced some new members for the church. Maxwell told me that, "We've had quite a few new folks come to be a part of our parish from both the volunteer pool and from the food line as well. People see what we're doing here and want to be a part of a church that does that kind of work."[22] She told me of one gentleman, a lapsed Catholic, who had lost his long-time partner and "came as a soup kitchen volunteer for about a year and then decided to check out the congregation. Not only did he join, but he has also done just about everything that one can do in our parish. He's a terrific leader."[23]

There's something enormously powerful and uniting about "Service. Period!" In addition to uniting an incredibly diverse group of people, it also seems to heal those who are in need of spiritual support. In my ministry through the years, I have done a great deal of premarital and marital counseling. When a couple comes to me at loggerheads and seemingly without hope, I will often send them on a Habitat build for a weekend or on a weeklong mission trip together. I do so because I have seen all kinds of relational brokenness healed by getting the couple *out of* the navel gaz-

21. Maxwell, interview.
22. Ibid.
23. Ibid.

ing and finger pointing that takes place in a counselor's office, and getting them *into* some no strings attached service to those who need it most.

I have come to trust in the transforming power of "Service. Period!" The Church of the Holy Apostles has come to trust in it too, and so has every one of the communities I have visited in the researching of this book. This power shouldn't surprise us, for it is what Jesus, himself, tapped into. He never attached conditions to his feeding, healing, or serving. If someone was hungry he fed him. If someone was thirsty he gave her drink. If someone was sick, he laid his hands upon him.

As the institutional church continues its downward spiral toward irrelevance, the resurrected communities of Christ's followers will thrive, at least in part, because of their Service. Period! They'll be in the business of doing Christlike things with no motive other than compassion. Such resurrection communities will also be extremely savvy about separating their missional endeavors from their overall budgets, in order to access funds and volunteer support from beyond their own communities. Several of the exemplary communities I visited had actually set up separate 501(c)(3)'s for their primary, on-going mission projects, enabling them to raise funds from a wealth of sources and to enlist non-Christians and non-religious organizations in their efforts. Broader partnerships with knowledgeable and effective organizations from both the corporate and non-profit spheres will be essential for those Christian communities seeking to make a difference in tomorrow's world. Perhaps these kinds of partnerships and budget innovations are what Jesus had in mind when he urged his followers to be "shrewd as snakes but innocent as doves."[24]

But anyone who dares to bear the name of Jesus simply must serve others as Jesus did, with no hidden agendas and no manipulative motives. Christian credibility is at all-time low, and the only way for communities of disciples to regain trust is to start doing what communities like Wicker Park Grace, Solomon's Porch, Glide, The Simple Way, and The Church of the Holy Apostles are doing: serving others—period!

QUESTIONS FOR DISCUSSION

1. What do you think of John Buchanan's prescription that "maybe there is no more important and life-giving strategy for every church than finding something Christlike to do"?

24. Matt 10:16, NIV.

2. Have you ever wondered whether "service to the least of these on its own is enough"? Jones believes, "there is a strong evangelical mind-set in many of us that causes us to question whether our good deeds to the poor are sufficient on their own, or whether they need to be supplemented with some sort of preaching or verbal explanation that includes the spoken name of Jesus." Do you struggle with such a mindset?

3. Is service why your community of faith exists? If so, does your budget reflect that? Does where your clergy and laity put their time and energy reflect that reason to exist?

4. Jones believes that "once we start meeting the needs of others *in order to* preach to or try to convert them, our service loses its Christ-likeness, its authenticity, and its legitimacy." What do you think? Why?

5. Gabe Lyons and David Kinnaman's book *unchristian* reveals that only "one third of young outsiders to the church believe that Christians genuinely care about them . . . Rather than being genuinely interested in people for their friendship, we (Christians) often seem like spiritual headhunters." Have you ever been "served" by someone with an ulterior motive? What does that feel like? Have you ever been served by someone who was "Serving. Period"? How did the two experiences compare?

6. What do you think about the way The Church of the Holy Apostles has used its sanctuary for the last twenty-some years? Can you envision your congregation doing something similar with its most sacred space? Why or why not?

7. At one point, Jones interviews a Jewish volunteer at the Holy Apostles' Soup Kitchen who says, Christians and Muslims "are on the very same page when it comes to serving others." Do you generally think of Judaism, Islam, and Christianity as being on the same page when it comes to serving others? Why or why not?

8. What do you think of Jones' assertion that vibrant communities of disciples will raise funds for serving others from a "wealth of sources" and even enlist "non-Christians and non-religious organizations in their efforts"? Have you and your faith community experimented with "broader partnerships" and sought out knowledgeable and effective organizations from both the corporate and non-profit spheres to help in your service efforts? Why or why not?

6

Getting Out of the Real Estate Business

The church is not a building
The church is not a steeple
The church is not a resting place
The church is a people

—Avery and Marsh[1]

May God deliver us from mindlessly adopting an edifice complex.

—Frank Viola[2]

First we shape our buildings. Thereafter, they shape us.

—Winston Churchill[3]

ONE SUNDAY DURING THE children's sermon, I asked all the kids and all the adults in the congregation to draw the first thing they thought of when I said the word "church." Every single kid and every single adult drew a church building, complete with a steeple. I followed that up by having the elementary school kids teach the congregation the "I am the Church, You are the Church, We are the Church together" song. We hammered hard on the verse that includes the phrase, "the church is not a building." But it was all to no avail. I continue to hear our entire congregation repeatedly say things like, "Are you coming to church next

---

1. Avery, Richard K. and Marsh, Donald S., "We are the Church," (Port Jervis: 1972).
2. Viola, Frank, *Reimagining Church*, 95.
3. Viola, Frank and Barna, George. *Pagan Christianity*, 44.

Sunday?" and "Our church is the big white one on the corner" or "Church was really great this morning!"

No matter how hard I've tried as a pastor, I've never gotten any of my flocks to distinguish the church from the church building. My chronic frustration at this reaches its boiling point every year at budget time. That is when, once again, I always have to come to terms with the fact that we, like most Christian congregations in this country, are spending the vast majority of our pledged dollars simply to keep our building going. We pay to heat it, clean it, re-roof it, carpet it, paint it, landscape it, and, despite the fact that we're located in northern Michigan, air condition it. By the time we and most congregations finish paying our monthly mortgages, utility bills, and maintenance fees, there's not a heck of a lot left to do many of the important things that Jesus did and told us to do. As Dustin McBride, twenty-three-year-old Co-founder and CEO of Acirfa (a company that works to get high quality, low-cost bikes to Zambia) puts it, "We, as a new generation, are tired of building bigger church buildings when we are called by God to look after the poor, the widows, the orphans, and those that suffer from injustice."[4]

There can be little doubt that in America the Church has become a building. But from both a biblical and an historical perspective, this ought not be the case. Our word "church" comes from the Greek word "*ecclesia*," meaning "gathering." *Ecclesia* carries no connotation whatsoever of a building. As Stanley Grenz puts it, "The choice of '*ecclesia*' as the designation of the Christian community suggests that the New Testament believers viewed the Church as neither an edifice nor an organization. They were a people—people brought together by the Holy Spirit—a people bound to each other through Christ."[5]

Gatherings of the followers of Jesus had been going on for centuries before there were ever buildings for them in which to gather. The first 300 years of Christian history offers neither biblical nor extra-biblical evidence of any buildings being built as churches. In fact, all the *ecclesias* were house gatherings, often held in secret. It wasn't until the reign of Constantine and his politically motivated, self-serving edict to make Christianity the official religion of his empire that so-called church buildings began to spring up.

4. McBride, "Enjoying the 'In-between' Times," *Sojourners*, June 2008, 23.

5. Grenz, *Reimagining Church*, 83.

"Almost overnight, an impressive architectural setting had to be created for the new official faith, so that the Church might be visible to all. Constantine himself devoted the full resources of his office to this task, and within a few years an astonishing number of large, empire-sponsored churches arose, not only in Rome but also in Constantinople, in the Holy Land, and at other important sites. These structures were a new type, now called the Early Christian basilica, that provided the basic model for the development of church architecture in Western Europe."[6]

While it might be easy to think of these new and impressive edifices as intended to honor God, it is probably more accurate to think of them as an effective way for the emperor to both keep an eye on and maintain authority over the growing Christian community.

As we move forward into the Renaissance period, European Christians began to build enormous cathedrals, many of which still stand today, though most are empty and unused, except as museums. These structures often took more than a hundred years to build and sought to cast the worshiper's eyes and thoughts heavenward. Obviously, buildings like these were extremely costly to build and were both few and far between. It was a huge status symbol for a town to have its own cathedral. Ken Follett's *Pillars of the Earth*, while fictional, does provide some helpful information about the cathedral period in Renaissance Christian history.

As we move forward in time to American Church history, it is probably the Puritans we should thank for the movement to have a church building at the center of every town. Early Puritan settlements were often built in a clearing with the church in the center and homes and businesses surrounding it. But we should keep in mind for our purposes that in such times there was only one church building per town. Nowadays, it is not uncommon to find a dozen church buildings in a town of only a few thousand people. Like the old cathedrals in Europe, however, more and more of today's churches are getting emptier rather than fuller, and some already lie vacant and unused.

If we include pre-Christian history in our look at the evolution of religious buildings, we could come away with the distinct impression that God has always been opposed to buildings in His honor. While David wanted to build a temple for the Lord, God dissuaded David, saying, "I have not lived in a house since the day I brought up the people of Israel

6. Davies, et al, *Jansen's History of Art: The Western Tradition*, 196.

from Egypt to this day, but I have been moving about in a tent and a tabernacle. Wherever I have moved with all the Israelites, did I ever say to any of their rulers whom I commanded to shepherd my people Israel, 'Why have you not built me a house of cedar?'"[7]

How many times was the temple in Jerusalem destroyed? The glorious and elaborate temple that Solomon built didn't last, nor did the one that Nehemiah rebuilt after the Babylonian exile. And then in 70 A.D., under Nero's empire, the temple of Jerusalem was burned to the ground. It was as if *Somebody* didn't want a building to be associated with almighty God. As the author of Luke/Acts would later have Paul put it, "The God who made the world and everything in it is the Lord of heaven and earth and does not live in temples built by human hands."[8]

Biblical history reminds us that there is neither precedent nor mandate for gathered communities of Christians to have their own buildings. Even as far back as the first 500 years of emerging Judaism, God was believed to dwell on mountains and in tents that moved with the people. Think of the Ark of the Covenant.

Moving into the early Christian period, there is nothing in the life or teachings of Jesus that suggests such structures were a part of God's design. In fact, Jesus' most famous remark about religious buildings was uttered when he was standing before the latest edition of the Jerusalem temple. Luke records it this way: "Some of his disciples were remarking about how the temple was adorned with beautiful stones and with gifts dedicated to God. But Jesus said, 'As for what you see here, the time will come when not one stone will be left on another; every one of them will be thrown down.'"[9] Elsewhere in the gospels, Jesus states it even more strongly and personally: "I will destroy this temple and raise it again in three days."[10]

In her recent work, *An Altar in the World,* Barbara Brown Taylor gets at our corrupt human need for buildings that contain God. "Do we build God a house so that we can choose when to go see God? Do we build God a house in lieu of having God stay at ours? Plus, what happens to the rest of the world when we build our four walls – even four gorgeous walls—

---

7. II Sam 7:6–7 NIV.

8. Acts 24:17 NIV.

9. Luke 21:5–6 NIV.

10. John 2:19 NIV.

cap them with a steepled roof, and designate *that* the House of God? What happens to the riverbanks, the mountaintops, the deserts, and the trees? What happens to the people who never show up in our houses of God?"[11] (p. 9) Brown Taylor concludes, "Without one designated place to make their offerings, people are set free to see the whole world as an altar."[12]

What, then, would communities of Christ followers be like if we didn't have buildings at all? What if Rev. Romal Tune of the Washington, D.C. based Clergy Strategic Alliances is right when he predicts that, "The church will in twenty years not be defined by a building that people attend for worship on Sunday morning, but by how Christians treat people in the world"?[13] What if new communities of Christ's followers were to reconfigure themselves with the commitment never to have buildings or property of any kind? A building-less congregation would, from the very beginning of its life together, be able to devote a huge percentage of its time, energy, and resources to others, particularly the poor and downtrodden. Imagine the power of a Christian community's witness if it were actually to give away more than it kept for itself, if it helped build houses for the homeless without having a home of its own. For far too long the Christian Church has given only its leftovers away and then retreated to our mansions on the hill. Such giving can't help but call into question the authenticity of our espoused commitment to the poor and our integrity as a Christ-inspired institution.

The story is told of an old rescue station and lighthouse that had, for years, lighted the way for boats around a precarious point of land. The keeper of the light and his fellow rescue workers had saved countless lives when ships found themselves outmatched by the mighty and unpredictable sea. These rescues often included bringing the sodden, bedraggled, and often wounded survivors back to the station. Such operations took their toll on the rescue station and lighthouse, not only dirtying it, but also wearing out the carpet, the furniture, etc. Over time, the board that oversaw the lighthouse and rescue mission thought it best to limit the number of rescues per year which the crew undertook and to relegate any wet and bloody survivors to one small corner of the station, so as to minimize the wear and tear on their historic facility. This went on for

11. Brown Taylor, *An Altar in the World*, 9.

12. Brown Taylor, 8.

13. Romal Tune, "Finding My Religion," by Amy Green in *Sojourners,* June 2008, 16–17.

a while, but soon the board of directors took stock of things again and decided to cease rescues altogether, in order to preserve their beautiful landmark rescue station as a members-only club for social events and cocktail parties.

Many outsiders and not a few conflicted insiders have come to view Christian congregations and their buildings as going the way of this lighthouse and rescue station, drifting further and further from their original purpose and mission in favor of existing strictly for themselves.

But let's not give our buildings away too quickly. After all, lots of American churches, including my own, have used our buildings to benefit so many in our communities. Twelve Step groups, community boards, food pantries, and, in some rare instances, even free clinics and homeless shelters have been housed in church buildings. Many Christian communities have been extremely generous with their buildings, truly reaching out to their communities while asking nothing in return. Without our own facilities, how could we ever have done such good and important work? This is a fair question, to be sure. But without buildings, communities of Christians might be more apt to build positive connections and relationships with schools, businesses, and other social service organizations, in order to find facilities to house our ministries. That would certainly give congregations an incentive to be more constructively plugged into their communities instead of being seen as arrogant, stand offish, and removed.

Most start-up churches begin without a facility, meeting in homes and halls or even renting space in a local school. But in America, it's almost as if a church isn't really a legitimate church until it has its *own* building, its *own* steeple, its *own* . . . its *own*. The American obsession with "Bigger is Better" may also have something to do with our inability even to conceive of a Christian community without a building. Fledgling communities soon outgrow the particular basement or living room in which they initially meet. Often even a classroom or gymnasium proves inadequate as numeric growth takes place.

But what if numeric growth isn't the point? What if new communities of Christ's followers formed with the understanding that when we outgrow the house or the hall, we'll start another small community on another block or on the other side of town? Frank Viola notes that when the first century Christian communities outgrew one home, "they simply multiplied and met in several other homes, following the 'house to house' principle."[14] Viola cites Acts 2:46 as proof of this: "Every day they continued to meet together in the temple courts. They broke bread in their homes and ate together with glad and sincere hearts, praising God and enjoying the favor of all people." If new resurrection communities form with an absolute commitment to serving the poor above all else, perhaps we will be zealous about minimizing our overhead and administrative costs. Perhaps we will be willing to build mutually beneficial alliances across religious lines instead of buildings. Perhaps we will be willing to be small and steady communities of integrity and service, instead of assimilators in a super-sized culture gone awry.

Of all the things a Christian community does, it is really only when we gather for worship that we truly require a large space. The traditional understanding of corporate worship requires that the entire community gather in one place and time on a weekly basis, and it makes perfect sense that a congregation would do so. But does this critical, corporate, once-a-week gathering truly warrant laying out all the resources to build a building for that sole purpose? During warm weather months, couldn't local parks, beaches, woods, and back yards provide ample and inspiring worship spaces? When an indoor, more protected space is required, schools, auditoriums, and businesses are possibilities. A fledgling new community in my area rents one of the movie theaters within a multi-theater complex for its weekly corporate gathering. There are a lot of empty, unused buildings on Saturday evenings and Sunday mornings. In New Testament times, "when it was necessary for the 'whole church' to gather together, the church in Jerusalem met in large settings such as the open courts of the temple and Solomon's porch."[15] Comparable meeting places in today's world might be a public park, pavilion, or the food court of a mall.

But as we move into a radically different paradigm for Christian communities, it might be time to rethink the very nature of corporate worship. For example, is working on a Habitat house worship? Could a Christian community meet for a series of Sunday mornings or Saturday evenings on site at a Habitat project, interspersing songs, prayers, and readings with their hammering and sawing? Is cleaning up a city park or a public beach an act of worship? Could a new kind of corporate worship take place in such public, free settings, while manual labor is being done? If so,

14. Viola, *Reimagining Church*, 85.

15. Ibid., 94

wouldn't this new kind of corporate gathering further reduce the need for a building owned and operated by a particular community of faith?

If we look at so many of the newer, thriving, non-denominational congregations, they all have buildings. The megachurches have *mega* buildings, some on a par with college campuses. Such grandeur seems to suggest great power, success, and stature in the community. But since when did Christ call his followers to grandeur, power, success and status? Clearly, many mega-churches give mega bucks to various missions, both locally and globally. But when their mission giving is viewed as a percentage of their overall budgets, they're still spending a lot more on themselves—their facilities and their internal programs—than they'll ever spend on others. George Barna and Frank Viola claim that U.S. churches alone own "more than $230 billion dollars worth of real estate. And much of that money is borrowed. Christians give between nine and eleven billion dollars a year to church buildings."[16] Such a spending pattern can only continue to do what it has always done, call into question the authenticity and integrity of our work in Christ's name.

It is understandably difficult for those of us raised in church buildings even to conceive of a functioning Christian community without them. But there is so much more we could do in Christ's name if we weren't saddled with the financial burden of these immense and resource-sucking edifices. Just as importantly, any of us who have spent any time on church boards and committees know how much time and deadening energy goes into dealing with controversies related to the building itself. In 1987, almost immediately after I was ordained, I presided over my first session meeting at my first church in the Chicago area. After opening with what I thought was a fabulous devotion and centering prayer, that church board commenced a fiery debate on whose responsibility it was to clean up after the coffee hour. I had no sooner gotten that vital, Christ-centered issue put to rest when I found myself refereeing a battle over the color of the new carpeting for the sanctuary. It's not just the money we Christians pour into our buildings that sucks the life out of our churches; it's the hours of human energy, stress, and interpersonal battles buildings create that are crippling our communities of faith. How many former church insiders are now outsiders because of one too many committee meetings spent on utterly trivial, building-related controversies?

16. Ibid., 89.

In his amazing book *New Monasticism: What it has to Say to Today's Church*, Jonathan Wilson-Hartgrove ties any hope for church renewal to what he calls "relocation." Drawing upon his experience in Iraq during the US occupation there, he concludes,

> Where we locate ourselves doesn't only change our perspective. It can also change the thing we see and our capacity to reimagine it . . . What I learned about location in Iraq is what the monastic tradition has known for hundreds of years: sometimes you have to relocate in order to really see the world and reimagine your role in it. That's why Antony went to the desert and Francis took to the streets. They knew something was wrong with the church, but they couldn't see any alternatives from where they were. Their location blinded them, holding their imagination captive.[17]

My geographic contexts for ministry in the institutional church have been in fairly affluent, safe neighborhoods. My congregations could live most of their lives without ever witnessing chronic poverty, a violent crime, or a homeless family with their own eyes. Wilson-Hartgrove's wisdom enabled me to see what a huge barrier our location was and had always been to our ability to live as authentic witnesses of Jesus. Of course, we would periodically beat the drum for one missional cause or another. We'd take mission trips for a week here or there and bring back pictures and stories. We did more than our share of check writing in an attempt to fulfill our obligation to the poor and oppressed. But ultimately the "out of sight, out of mind" principle would win out. Our minds, lives, and expressions of faith were always most heavily influenced by what we saw day in and day out and, more importantly, by what we *didn't* see day in and day out. I'm reminded of what George H. Bush said when, during his reelection bid in 1992, he was asked about the growing plight of America's poor. He said, "The people I see when I look around every day are doing pretty good." I remember thinking, "Are you talking about your neighbors who share the same ocean view you have from your Kennebunkport summerhouse? Or are you referring to your millionaire neighbors who look out on those same rolling hills you do from your Texas ranch? I'm sure your view of the constantly manicured White House lawn and garden must look pretty good. But that's *not* America, President Bush. You need

---

17. Wilson-Hartgrove, *New Monasticism*, 76–77.

to get out of your limousines and mansions to see how more than half of your fellow countrymen live."

President Bush's problem, in my view, was a problem of location. That same problem has plagued America's churches, particularly as Christians have joined in the flight from urban areas to the greener, safer pastures of suburbia. I have the highest regard for those congregations who have chosen to remain downtown to minister among the folks who have no choice but to stay. Unfortunately, numerically speaking, those churches committed to their urban settings are few and far between here in the U.S.A. I have even more respect for people like Chris Haw and his wife Cassie, who have moved into a crime ridden, poor neighborhood, reclaimed and refurbished an abandoned home, and started an intentional Christian community there. Several other individuals and couples have followed the Haw's lead, moving their lives into the heart of a triangular block in Camden, New Jersey, where they have united with an existing Catholic parish down the street. Rather than building a new church building, Camden Community House has made use of abandoned homes and shared in the existing work of a Catholic church.

There are plenty of compelling reasons for new communities of Christians to give a building-less existence a chance. First, in a time when our integrity and reputation are at an all time low and when the rest of the world looks at us as judgmental, out-of-touch hypocrites, a huge and radical step like becoming voluntarily homeless might help people give Jesus another look. Second, given our current economic downturn, already being compared to the Great Depression, every church could stand to reduce its overhead. Third, the opportunity to build mutually beneficial relationships with other building owners—whether they are educators, business folk, professionals, or people of other denominations or faiths—would be tremendously promising in a constantly shrinking and pluralistic society. Fourth, ask anyone who has been a part of a start-up church about the early days in their development, and you will hear a wistful longing for the days when "we were still meeting in each others' homes" or "at the local school." There is a powerful and deeply spiritual intimacy available only to those small and simple communities, an intimacy that Christians have sacrificed on the altar of "Bigger is Better." Perhaps the time has come for Christians to transform our concept of "big," moving it away from the size of our buildings and toward the size and number of our opportunities to serve in a world of boundless human suffering.

Fifth, a Christian community without a building can constantly relocate itself, moving its base of operations to guarantee that its participants see and respond to the truly and chronically poor, the abandoned, and the forgotten.

If we were willing to take the difficult and disciplined steps to become building-less once again, I believe we would experience a second Pentecost, a spiritual and missional awakening that would reflect the very glory of the Son. A time is coming when building-burdened congregations will be forced to sell off our physical assets. To get out ahead of this inevitable curve and simplify our congregational lives by choice rather than necessity would authenticate our witness to the Son of man who "had no place to lay his head."[18]

I have been in contact for the last several years with a fairly new community of disciples that has made building-lessness their reality. It is the Community Church of Lake Forest/Lake Bluff in suburban Chicago. The Rev. Dr. Tom Dickelman founded this community ten years ago. For three months a year, the CCLFLB takes advantage of God's own temple for their worship gatherings—the beach. People bring lawn chairs and blankets and walk down the many stairs to one of the north shore's most pristine beaches. There is no cost for the use of this prime real estate, and the parishioners wouldn't meet anywhere else, particularly after suffering through the interminable Chicago winters.

For the other nine months each year, the CCLFLB rents the beautiful Lake Forest College Chapel on the campus of their local college. "We pay seventy five bucks a week for the building for thirty-six Sundays a year. So that comes to $2,700 of total building costs in our annual budget. Our people don't have to pay for its upkeep or worry about what to do when the furnace gives out or the roof needs repair. It's a pretty sweet deal for us, and it helps the college too, because their chapel is often just sitting empty."[19] Dickelman reports that his flock has absolutely no plans to ever build or purchase their own building. "There's no reason to. There is so much available real estate that is under used. And besides, we have much

18. Luke 9:58 NIV.

19. Tom Dickelman, interview by author, tape recording, Chicago, IL., April 21, 2009.

more important things to do with our financial resources."[20] Three years ago, the Community Church of Lake Forest/Lake Bluff started a charity called KidsUganda, and in that time they've already delivered over $2.5 million dollars in direct aid to Uganda. Over thirty participants in the CCLFLB community (roughly 15 percent of their people) have already been to Uganda, and no fewer than three more trips are in the planning stages. The Community Church also uses its time and money to serve its own local community as well, from sponsoring a Fourth of July Family Fair to creating The Lake Center, an innovative, subsidized counseling and human services program.

I have had the privilege of both attending and preaching at this innovative and building-less community. Despite their fledgling status, they have managed to assemble a worship band that could easily fill in for Paul Schaefer's all-star line-up on the Letterman Show. They play everything from upbeat arrangements of traditional hymns to stylized jazz, and from Chicago blues to R&B, and they do it all whether they're inside or out. "We are more interested in *soulful* music than that considered 'religious,'" offered Dickelman. "And that pretty much swings the musical doors wide open."[21]

"We never know what genre of music we're going to get here on Sunday," one enthused parishioner said the Sunday I preached there. "We just know it's going to be good!" Such outstanding yet informal music coupled with Dickelman's tremendous ease as a leader sets the tone for an authentic experience of God through worship. A visitor to CCLFLB is also sure to notice the focused energy and genuine compassion that is expended on the "Joys and Concerns" portion of worship. This time of sharing prayer requests is truly owned by the entire congregation.

Dickelman has kept the community extremely lean, with little overhead or excess. They rent a tiny storefront for the church office and meeting space, though, as Dickelman says, "We don't do a lot of meetings here." He added without apology, "In fact, the church only has one committee."[22] He doesn't believe in trying to be all things to all people or in offering a bunch of programs that folks don't really want or need anyway.

"Since we held our first service nearly ten years ago, I've called us 'a micro church,'" said Dickelman. "We don't offer all the programs of many

20. Ibid.
21. Ibid.
22. Ibid.

bigger churches, but what we do—particularly worship and outreach—
we strive to do very well. We also don't involve people in ways that don't
add value, spiritual and otherwise, to their lives. People are so busy. They
already go to enough meetings. If we're going to ask them to do anything,
it had better be meaningful enough, rich enough, and fulfilling enough to
warrant their investment of time and self."[23] In examining the CCLFLB's
annual budget, they are staying true to their word, and it is obvious that
this young community's outreach efforts have benefited tremendously
from being unencumbered by building debt.

The Community Church of Lake Forest/Lake Bluff has created a
model to which the rest of us ought to be paying attention. Making use
of existing facilities, whether natural or man-made, at a fraction of the
cost, and then being freed up to do significant, substantive service to the
community and world creates a witness that is compelling to both the
churched and the un-churched.

There are contexts and communities, however, in which having one's
own building might be necessary, particularly in poor, urban areas, where
children are not safe on the streets. But those of us who live in relative
safety and security would do well to divest ourselves from the real estate
market and invest much more heavily in the Jesus business of feeding the
poor, taking care of the orphan and the widow, visiting the sick and the
imprisoned, and working for justice. The amount of money we church folk
have spent on ourselves and our own comfort in the name of Christian
faith is both excessive and embarrassing. The rest of the world has taken
notice and has wisely been pulling the plug on funding our endeavors,
taking their charitable dollars elsewhere.

Living Vision, the community I have begun in Northern Michigan,
has made it a part of our charter never to have a building. Our only real
estate is some donated land we're using for a cooperative farm. We look forward to the adventure of being a community that is joyfully and intentionally homeless, even in the depths of a Northern Michigan winter. We think
Joni Mitchell was onto something when she included these words in her hit
song, "Woodstock:" "Got to get back to the land to set my soul free."

We don't see ourselves as making any sacrifices by going building-
less. We're extremely excited about all that God has in store for us as a

23. Ibid.

journeying people, as a flexible body that can relocate constantly in the spirit of Jonathan Wilson-Hartgrove's New Monasticism movement.

Who knows? Perhaps one day an American preacher will give all the kids and adults in her congregation a piece of paper and pencil and ask them all to draw the first thing they picture when they hear the word "church." And perhaps that congregation will draw things like a car pulling over to help a person with a flat tire; a person stopping to tend to a beaten man on the roadside; a group of people huddled in prayer together; a medical team giving immunizations to at risk children; or a woman visiting a prisoner behind bars. Maybe someday . . .

QUESTIONS FOR DISCUSSION

1. As you read through the history of church buildings, what did you find yourself thinking? Do you agree with Jones' conclusion that "there is neither precedent nor mandate for gathered communities of Christians to have their own buildings"?

2. Discuss Barbara Brown Taylor's questions and their suggested implications: "Do we build God a house so that we can choose when to go see God? Do we build God a house in lieu of having God stay at ours? Plus, what happens to the rest of the world . . . What happens to the riverbanks, the mountaintops, the deserts, and the trees? What happens to the people who never show up in our houses of God?"

3. Jones asks us to "imagine the power of a Christian community's witness if it were actually to give away more than it kept for itself, if it helped build houses for the homeless without having a home of its own." Discuss this radical vision of a modern day *ecclesia*. Is it even possible? What would it take for your community of faith to reconfigure itself in this way?

4. Have you ever felt that your congregation has bought into America's "Bigger is Better" principle? What gets lost when numeric growth becomes the bottom line in a faith community? Reflect back to Chapter 2's emphasis on discipleship. Does apprenticeship to Jesus entail building bigger and bigger churches? Why or why not?

5. Of all the things a Christian community does, Jones notes that "it's really only when we gather for worship that we truly require a large space." He then asks a very provocative question: "Does this critical, corporate, once-a-week gathering truly warrant laying out all the

resources to build a building for that sole purpose?" What do you think and why?

6. Before your next group meeting, assign someone the task of getting a copy of your church's budget and bringing enough copies to the next meeting for everyone. Spend some time analyzing the numbers with a particular eye on building related expenses.

7. Jones argues that "it's not just the money we Christians pour into our buildings that sucks the life out of our churches; it's the hours of human energy, stress, and interpersonal battles which buildings create that are crippling our communities of faith." Debate this point within the group. Whenever possible, use examples from your own experience.

8. What do you think of Jonathan Wilson-Hartgrove's concept of "relocation"? Have you ever considered that being permanently rooted in one particular location might be keeping you from seeing with the eyes of Jesus? Discuss what your particular location has kept you from seeing. How might that limitation affect your mission and service?

9. What did you think of the way The Community Church of Lake Forest/Lake Bluff has navigated its buildingless-ness?

7

A Return to Tent-making

Writing Myself Out of a Job

I BELIEVE WITH ALL my heart that future communities of Christ follow-ers, seeking to live and serve in their Rabbi's image, will do so *without* paid, professional leaders or pastors. Why would I suggest such a radical change from the status quo, particularly when I have drawn a wonderful salary from the churches I've served? At the most crass level, it's simple economics. As Elaine Heath, Perkins School of Theology professor, sug-gests in her work, *The Mystic Way of Evangelism,* "Increasing numbers of small churches cannot afford a full-time pastor and are opting instead for part-time, bivocational clergy."[1] She reached this conclusion not only as an academician, but as one who served several small Methodist churches in Ohio. "I saw how much my congregations struggled to pay and support me, and I began to wonder, 'Does a congregation really exist to support its pastor or to bless and serve the world?'"[2]

It's not only small churches that are being forced to consider bivo-cational pastors. Even in the upper-middle class congregation I served for seven years, once we finished paying for the building along with staff salaries and benefits each year—particularly health care—there was very little left to devote to the real work of a Christian church, things like feed-ing the hungry, taking care of the poor, and caring for the least of these.

In most any church's budget, by far its two biggest line items will be building expenses and personnel expenses. These two skyrocketing ex-penses have hog-tied the Christian Church, making it virtually impossible for Christ's followers to fulfill our assigned mission in any significant way.

1. Heath, *The Mystic Way of Evangelism,* 33.
2. Elaine Heath, interview by author, tape recording, Santa Fe, NM., 28 July, 2009.

But beyond the merely practical, economic considerations, the bivocational pastoral model has a strikingly clear Biblical history as well. "Jesus and the apostles were all working people. Paul was as well," Dr. Heath notes, and she is not alone in this perspective.[3] Frank Viola and George Barna remind us that the notion of a distinct classification of clergy with which so many of us were raised is not even biblical in the first place. "Should we support an office and a role that has no basis in the New Testament?"[4] There really is only one verse in all of the Christian scriptures—Ephesians 4:11—that even mentions the role of pastor, and that verse does so in the context of listing the various equal roles for which God has equipped ordinary people to fulfill. Paul writes, "It was he who gave some to be apostles, some to be prophets, some to be evangelists, and some to be pastors and teachers, to prepare God's people for works of service . . ."[5]

In the Book of Acts, our best chronicle of the early church, there is no mention whatsoever of the pastoral office. Even when we examine the earliest and most famous church planter, the Apostle Paul himself, we find that he did not receive money from the churches he established, but instead met his own expenses through his profession of tent-making. "You yourselves know that these hands of mine have supplied my own needs and the needs of my companions. In everything I did, I showed you that by this kind of hard work we must help the weak, remembering the words Jesus himself said, 'it is more blessed to give than to receive.'"[6]

Moving beyond the first century of the Common Era, we can see that the birth of the professional clergy didn't commence until after Cyprian, after the Council of Nicea in 325, and after Constantine granted so many privileges to pastors in the latter part of the fourth century. This emerging clergy class then grew to even greater prominence in the Middle Ages, a time when the vast majority of church folk were illiterate and uneducated. The pastor in medieval times was often the most educated person in the town or even the only one who could read and had access to the scriptures. Church members in the Middle Ages needed an educated expert to read and interpret the scriptures for them and to lead them in the way of Christ.

3. Heath, interview.
4. Barna, Viola, *Pagan Christianity*, 143.
5. Ephesians 4:11 NIV.
6. Acts 20:33–35 NIV.

Today's world, however, is a very different one, indeed. Certainly, in most American congregations, the vast majority of members are not only literate, but are often every bit as educated as their pastor. While the pastor's degree may have a more biblical or theological focus, today's lay people have access to many, if not all, of the books, courses, and materials to which their pastor has been exposed. Thanks to Christian publishing companies like Baker Books and Zondervann and to lay training offered by organizations like Willow Creek and Group, the people in the pews have terrific opportunities to equip themselves for service in Christian communities. Even seminary degrees are now available on-line and through non-traditional, off-campus programs of study. There are hundreds of organizations that have made it very easy and affordable for lay people to receive training to lead Bible studies, preach sermons, organize mission trips, and even plant churches. We ordained clergy are no longer the only ones capable of leading a congregation the way we once were.

But there is an even more compelling reason Christians need to open themselves to bivocationalism, and that is the emerging commitment to genuine discipleship and missional living we are witnessing in younger generations of Christians. Professor Heath notes that, "While the traditional Church will continue to exist with its full-time pastors, the emerging missiological context will lead us toward more and more bivocational ministries—small communities of prayer, practice, and prophetic living led by teams of bivocational pastors."[7] These teams of pastors, according to Heath, will serve in a self-emptying way, in keeping with the "kenosis" which Paul praises in Philippians 2. "Rather than a church focusing its energy and resources on itself (pastors' salaries and benefits, big buildings with massive utility bills, programs to keep church members happy), the future church will focus its resources outward in service . . . The world needs to see a church that is not all about itself," Heath concludes.[8] It is the world's need for an authentic, other-serving kind of community that will fuel the difficult but necessary transition from professional clergy to bivocational ministry.

It was for all these reasons that in the summer of 2009, I made the very difficult decision to leave my well paying, pension and benefits providing position in a Presbyterian church in order to found an alternative

7. Heath, interview.
8. Heath, *The Mystic Way of Evangelism*, 134.

Christian community, which, by design, will never pay me a cent. I am no hero for doing this. At best, I am finding a way to give back after years of being generously compensated by communities that probably should have been feeding the poor and housing the homeless instead of picking up the tab for my salary, pension, and benefits package.

At the time of my departure, my very generous, mission-minded church was spending 93 percent of its annual budget on building costs and personnel expenses. That hardly seems justifiable for a community claiming to follow Jesus, the one who had no place to lay his own head.[9] And so, when I left to start a different kind of spiritual community, I vowed that I would never take money from the community I served. In order to do this, I had to leave more than my particular church; I had to say goodbye to the entire traditional denominational structure of which I had been a part for most of my life. My denomination literally had no idea what to do with the seven principles I articulate in this book. But what seemed radical to my Presbytery in the summer of 2009 will soon become practical necessity, as new economic realities and well-documented demographic trends force congregations to do far more than merely tighten their belts. I believe that in the coming years, those who seek to lead authentic communities in the way of Jesus, will take very similar steps to the ones I've taken, freeing their congregations and communities for more fruitful, lay led service to others.

It is not easy for me to speak against a tradition from which I benefited for so many years. And the conviction out of which I speak should not be taken as a slight to professional pastors. I am in no way suggesting that the professional clergy are the roots of all Church evil, nor that we have been completely ineffective as leaders. Often it has been a trained member of the clergy in a congregation who has helped that community know Christ more deeply and undertake his mission more faithfully. Effective pastors have launched Bible studies, mission trips, and outreach efforts, all of which can contribute to the building of God's kingdom. But I feel, as Elaine Heath does, the call of the Holy Spirit to study and move toward a new—or perhaps very ancient—way of both being and leading the church in 2009 and beyond.

Those who find it impossible to imagine a clergy-less church would do well to study the history and effectiveness of the Alcoholics

9. Matt 8:20 NIV.

Anonymous movement. It was in 1935 that Bill Wilson and Bob Smith crafted the Twelve Steps. In addition to their underlying assumption that it was God who would lead the addict through recovery, they also assumed from the start, writes Phyllis Tickle, "that the addicted were better, more effective healers of the addicted than were the non-addicted experts and authorities, including pastors and clerics. Now help—effective, productive, demonstrable help—was coming from other, equally wounded and empathetic non-professionals." Tickle concludes that, "AA and its success, however unintentionally, delivered a serious blow to the role and authority of the clergy in this country."[10]

I have significant personal experience in both Alanon and Adult Children of Alcoholics, which are Twelve Step programs. My healing and growth in these exemplary lay-led groups has been monumental, and the overall experience has opened me to the notion of a lay-led church as well. Writer and theologian Frederick Buechner's description of AA rings true for me.

> They have no hierarchy. They have no dues or budget. They do not advertise or proselytize. Having no buildings of their own, they meet wherever they can. Nobody lectures them and they do not lecture each other . . . Sometimes one of them will take special responsibility for another—to be available at any hour of day or night if the need arises. There's not much more to it than that, and it seems to be enough . . . You can't help thinking that something like this is what the Church is meant to be and maybe once was before it got to be Big Business.[11]

Henry Nouwen's groundbreaking work *The Wounded Healer* has also been formative for me in the way I function as a pastor, as one who helps the folks in our congregation identify and lay claim to their own gifts, so that they can lead others in ministry.

In many ways the move toward a lay-led, tent making pastoral model has already begun and taken root. More and more of my most respected preacher colleagues are turning to their congregations for guidance as they prepare the Sunday message. Every Tuesday, Doug Pagitt, founding pastor of Solomon's Porch in the Twin Cities, holds an open Bible study/discussion focusing on the passage for the upcoming Sunday. "In many

10. Tickle, *The Great Emergence*, 92–93.

11. Buechner, *Listening to Your Life*, 205–6.

ways this group sets the form, feel, and content for what will happen on Sunday night during our worship gathering," Pagitt says, "so that when the same passage is presented to the larger group, it will be clear that it has been wrestled with not just by the theologian who gives the sermon, but by 'regular' people as well."[12]

Speaking of 'regular people,' perhaps the best reason of all for Christian communities to return to the tent-making model of ministry is so they can do away with the distance that has emerged between clergy and laity. So many folks in the pews have always struggled with a sense of distance from their pastor, who has presumed to preach to them without really knowing what it's like to walk in their shoes, to have to find a job, or to earn a living outside the church. Even the most dedicated, plugged-in church volunteers must wonder from time to time whether their pastor really grasps that they and their families are giving what they're giving to the church on top of full time jobs, countless family and community commitments, and everything else that it takes to run a household in today's rapid-fire culture. We professional pastors and paid church staff get compensated to go to church meetings, to run our programs, to visit people in the hospital, and even to show up on Sunday mornings. We have no other work to do. If the pastor of a church were truly in same boat as every one of his/her parishioners, what might that do to morale and the sense of everyone serving as equals in ministry together? What might that do to a pastor's credibility within a congregation?

In my own congregations, I found that we who were paid staff could be incredibly judgmental toward our lay leaders and volunteers. When one of our elders or deacons didn't make it to a meeting or missed a deadline, paid staffers could be brutal in our criticism of the "uncommitted," "slacking" layperson. I constantly had to remind myself and fellow staffers that this very lay leader with whom we were disappointed was a volunteer, a volunteer whom we are lucky to have working with us in ministry at all, given that she had a full-time job, is raising three children, and served several boards and organizations, only one of which was at our church. I can't help but believe that if we pastors were tent-makers—having to earn our livings outside the church like everyone else—we would be a lot more respectful toward and appreciative of our lay people for whatever time and energy they were able to offer our community.

12. Pagitt, *Reimagining Spiritual Formation*, 87.

But ultimately, it is the mission of Christ's church that has suffered most at the hands of professional pastors and the sacerdotalism that has accompanied us. Personnel expenses have increased exponentially, crippling church budgets and leaving little or no resources to offer meaningful help to the downtrodden or to fulfill any of the other truly missional functions with which Jesus charged us. Imagine for a moment what your church would be able to do missionally if it no longer had to pay for a building, nor any personnel expenses. Think about the amount of dollars that would be freed up, and think about the kinds of things you and your community might choose to do with those dollars.

So the question is am I willing to forego my salary and benefits and find another job, while serving my faith community as an equal rather than as a superior? Given that I see today's Church as both far from what Christ intended it to be and heading for almost certain extinction, I have gradually become willing to be a tent-making pastor. I am finally able to join Paul in saying to my current family of faith, "You yourselves know that these hands of mine have supplied my own needs and the needs of my companions. In everything I did, I showed you that by this kind of hard work we must help the weak, remembering the words Jesus himself said, 'it is more blessed to give than to receive.'"[13]

I want to invite any and all professional pastors out there to join me in voluntarily becoming tent-makers. I think it would be a huge statement of our faith and of our desire to reflect Jesus in all we do. And to you pastors who are not yet willing to make this risky, paradigmatic shift from professional clergy to tent-maker, mark my words: this change is likely to be forced upon you due to the simple and stark economics of today's Church. In fact, in poorer churches and communities in my state and in my denomination, it's already happening. Of the forty-two congregations I oversaw as Moderator of The Presbytery of Mackinac, fifteen had no full-time ordained pastor and five shared a pastor with at least one other congregation. In the larger denomination nation wide, 45 percent of all Presbyterian congregations were without installed pastoral leadership in 2007 and that number continues to grow. *Presbyterians Today* Magazine notes that most of the vacancies "are in small churches with small budgets, many in out-of-the-way places."[14] John Bolt's article goes on to report that

13. Acts 20:33–35 NIV.
14. Bolt, "No pastor? No problem," in *Presbyterians Today*, June 2009, 13.

small churches are becoming more innovative and flexible about how they lead themselves—rotating preachers, using a Commissioned Lay Pastor, or just doing it themselves. Elaine Heath from Perkins School of Theology argues that, "In poor communities it has always been bivocational ministry; we just haven't honored it in the larger Church. Additionally, with the financial crisis that came to the surface in October of 2008, churches will see their largest, most reliable givers—retirees and the 65 and over crowd—forced to decrease their pledges significantly."[15]

Believe it or not, I see this forthcoming inevitable return to tentmaking as a very positive development in the history of Christ's followers. Once we work through the challenging logistics of this monumental adjustment and begin to execute its prescribed transitions, we will see some stunning developments in the missional impact these post-Church congregations can have, both upon their communities and upon the larger world. Imagine taking an offering during a weekly worship service and then having the luxury to decide together what you'd like to do with that week's offering—not just some of it, but *all* of it!

Emergent Church leader Tony Jones tells a wonderful story about some spontaneous giving that took place in his congregation, Solomon's Porch in Minneapolis.

> Two of my friends from South Africa were in Minnesota for the weekend and wanted to visit our church . . . During the five o'clock worship gathering Doug (the pastor) invited Deon and Eugene to talk a bit about what they do and why they were touring emergent churches in the United States. After a few minutes, Doug asked how Solomon's Porch could support them and pray for them. Deon said that one of the things he's trying to do is buy bicycles for kids who live in townships. 'One boy I know wants to go to art school,' Deon told us, 'but it's five miles each way and he has to walk with art supplies. I'd love to get him a bike.' My wife Julie punched me in the arm. 'Let's buy a bike.' 'You mean us?' I asked. But as I was asking, she was pulling the stocking cap off her head. 'Doug,' she said above the crowd as people were gathering to lay hands on Deon and Eugene and pray for them, 'I'm going to pass my hat to raise money for a bike for that boy.' . . . She dropped in a twenty-dollar bill . . . Meanwhile, I was thinking how truly odd this was. Never, I thought, have I been a part of a church where anyone can stand up in the middle of a service and pass the hat for something. Julie

---

15. Heath, interview.

would have gotten tossed out of some churches for that behavior, or at least a reprimand since all fundraising efforts must be approved in triplicate by the missions committee—because if any old person with a pet project gets up and asks for money, the wheels will come off! Not to mention that it might adversely affect the weekly offering! But no one—not even the pastor—batted an eye when Julie passed the hat. It seemed not a bit unusual. And ten minutes later, when the hat got back to Julie, the 150 or so people in the room had contributed $307. Deon told us that would buy bikes for two or three children. At the 7:00 gathering, no one had a hat, so they passed a cowboy boot. And they raised even more.[16]

It's almost impossible for church folk to imagine the kind of freedom Jones describes at Solomon's Porch, that kind of hands-on, spontaneous, missional capability. And it's not just the money that would be freed up in a building-less, clergy-less model; it's the energy as well, energy that has been burned up over the years, as well-intentioned men and women have bickered endlessly about the color of carpeting, the dedication of the stained glass windows, the need for a new roof, or the best, most affordable health care plan for the pastor. If you talk to the millions of de-churched folks in America to find out why they no longer want anything to do with the church, it will often be because of the bickering about petty things that went on in their former church week after week. Or it might also be that the church seemed far more focused on maintaining and protecting its building and staff than on caring for the poor and the least of these in their own community.

I believe that once congregations produce budgets which are no longer dominated by building costs and personnel expenses, they will begin to see an outpouring of generosity and tithing like we have never seen before in the traditional, clergy led Church. It is to those Christian communities who have virtually no overhead and no administrative expenses that people will be drawn to give most generously. People with hearts shaped by Jesus will be excited to give to projects that reflect Jesus' own priorities—the feeding of the hungry, the clothing of the naked, the lifting up of the poor, and even the buying of a bike for the poor art student in Africa.

16. Jones, *The New Christians*, 211.

~

The future is going to be an exciting time in which to be a Christian. I see no reason to wait around for such a future when we can hasten its coming by choosing to live more biblically now.

On Tuesday, May 12, 2009, NBC's Today Show did a feature on St. Francis Parish in Scituate, Massachusetts. St. Francis was one of the many Catholic churches ordered closed by the Archdiocese of Boston back in 2004. Diocesan officials actually chain locked the doors of St. Francis before the people even had a chance to say goodbye to their church home. The feisty and faithful folks from St. Francis rebelled, refusing to comply with the sudden closure. They broke into the church to continue doing what they had done for generations, except for the fact that they didn't have a priest to help them do it. As a part of closing St. Francis, the priest who had been serving Scituate was transferred, and, of course, the Archdiocese wasn't about to send this renegade, unauthorized community another one.

The point of the Today Show piece was that this congregation went right on functioning without a priest and is still functioning that way today, five years after getting closed down! Members of the parish have stepped up to lead in all kinds of amazing ways. In fact, the only thing they haven't been able to do is the actual Mass. Out of respect for traditional Catholic beliefs, the folks at Scituate Parish have not served each other the bread and cup. What they have done in their priest-less church is experienced a total rejuvenation of their faith.

One parishioner, a Ms. Rogers I believe, reported that since the closure, the people of St. Francis are now "living their faith . . . walking it twenty-four hours a day, seven days a week, and it's amazing!" A fellow parishioner, a Ms. O'Brien, said of the Archdiocese's attempted closure, "They've created a monster and it's wonderful!"

The effect of running the church on their own—without a priest— has been nothing short of transformational. One man in the interview noted that he used to show up every Sunday unable to come up with the names of his fellow parishioners. Now he recognizes the faces, the families their from, and has no trouble with their names. "This has strengthened us," he said.

How ironic that when the very ingredient we've thought for centuries was an absolute necessity—the professional pastor—is taken away, the congregation begins to truly thrive and grow! What if the unintended result of having a distinct and professional class of clergy has been to create a passive laity that is largely unaware of their own gifts and abilities to lead?

I believe that the time has come to unleash the power and potential of the people in the pews by doing away with the Christian caste system of clergy and laity, ordained and un-ordained, paid and unpaid. While the reasons for this shift may, on the surface, seem economic, they are, in fact, deeply spiritual, ethical, and biblical as well. All kinds of hierarchies have come crumbling down, as our world has grown increasingly "flat," to use the language of Thomas Friedman.[17] The corporate world has seen unprecedented improvement and innovation, as workers have been empowered to make decisions and initiate substantive change. The companies that have fought this global movement by clinging to a top-down management style have gone the way of General Motors. Will the Church be next to declare Chapter 11 and hope for a government bailout?

Professor Heath's question should continue to ring in all our minds: "Does a congregation really exist to support their pastor or to bless and serve the world?"[18] There is no doubt in my mind that vital communities of Christ followers in the years to come will be blessing and serving the world without a paid, professional leader at the helm. This is why I have set up our Living Vision community experiment with no provision for paying me. Living Vision will not exist to support me. I will do what everyone else in the community is doing, finding employment wherever I can and offering myself to our spiritual community with no financial strings attached.

So far, in my first nine months of earning my living through three and sometimes four part-time jobs, I have learned a ton that is already making me a better, more sensitive pastor. I have pulled weeds and washed yachts for the rich, as they have looked down on me as an inferior. I've cared for an eighty-eight year old widow by taking her sailing. I've also taught developmental writing to community college students who aren't yet ready for the college level English curriculum. All these things I've been doing for a fraction of the income I once earned in the church. But somehow the work seems invaluable, humbling, and right.

---

17. Friedman, *The World is Flat*, title.

18. Heath, interview.

Who knows how our Northern Michigan experiment in spiritual community will fare? I certainly don't. But I do take great comfort in the assurance that this model for gathering disciples cannot fail financially. There is no minimum number of participants needed to get this experiment off the ground or to pay our bills. If we have four families, we'll flesh out our seven principles with those four families. If we have forty, we'll be Christ's disciples with forty. What we will never do, however, is be driven by financial concerns and considerations, for we have already seen where that way of doing things leads. I'm also buoyed by the fact that I will lead Living Vision without taxing the participants and without separating myself from them through a title or office.

Still, it won't be easy for anyone to let go of the long-established model of a professionally led Christian community, as it hasn't been easy for me. Many will fight this change for all kinds of reasons. But the world around the institutional Church has changed far too much for us to continue to prop up a model that divides people into two distinct and unequal classes. There are good men and good women across this country already leading faith communities as tent-makers, and more of us are joining their ranks every day, be it by choice or by necessity. And there are also countless others out there who, though they haven't had the opportunity to attend seminary, are infinitely capable of leading a community of disciples. I believe it will do spiritual communities immeasurable good to be led by one of their own, someone who "does not count equality with God something to be grasped, but empties him/herself, taking the form of a servant."[19]

19. Phil 2:6–7 RSV.

QUESTIONS FOR DISCUSSION

1. Professor Elaine Heath of Perkins School of Theology asks, "Does a congregation really exist to support its pastor or to bless and serve the world?" Do you see this as an either/or proposition? Why or why not? How will a congregation know when supporting its pastor(s) has gotten in the way of blessing and serving the world?

2. Have you ever considered the fact that there is no biblical basis for professional pastors? Why do you think this model of leading churches has endured for so long? What are its benefits and its drawbacks?

3. What did you think of the actions of the parishioners from St. Francis Parish in Scituate, Mass? Can you see how such an experience could be so spiritually fruitful for the people who have stepped up to lead in the priest's place?

4. Have you ever been challenged to look at yourself as a potential leader within your faith community? Imagine if your congregation didn't have a pastor. What ministry might you lead?

5. Have you ever gone through a temporary vacancy in your pulpit, such as an interim period between one pastor leaving and another one coming? If so, what do you remember about how the congregation responded to that void in leadership? Do you remember it as a negative or positive time for your faith community? Why?

6. Tony Jones of Solomon's Porch tells the story of his wife standing up right in the middle of a Sunday service to pass her hat in support of a mission that their guest speaker was spearheading. Have you ever experienced anything like this in your community of faith? If not, what do you think keeps your congregation from acting spontaneously?

7. If your congregation moved to a bivocational model of ministry, how would that affect the way you looked at and related to your pastor? Would the fact that he/she was working another full time or several part time jobs just to be able to keep serving you have significance for you? Why or why not?

Conclusion

Living the Vision & Common Threads

C AN A GROUP OF Christ followers unite around the practices of open theology, authentic discipleship, embracing risk, radical inclusiveness, Service. Period!, no paid leader, and intentional homelessness? Can these seven principles be lived in a coherent and joyful fashion by a community of seekers? Are there even any Christians out there who would want to be a part of such a radical alternative to the institutional Church, or is this just another utopian pipe dream?

These are the questions with which I am living at the present time. I have posed them to groups and individuals throughout my corner of Northern Michigan, and, through this book and its associated speaking engagements, to people all across the country. Anyone who wants to participate in this on-going dialogue is invited to visit and comment on my blog at: http://faith4tomorrow.blogspot.com

Living Vision is the community we have begun building in Harbor Springs, Michigan in attempt to offer a meaningful, authentic path to those seeking an apprenticeship in the Way of Jesus. We are an experimental community, a work in progress, still curious about where this road and these seven principles will take us. Our hope is that our lives, both individually and collectively, will come to more fully resemble the life of Jesus. As we journey together, we believe we will make a positive difference in Northern Michigan as well.

As the Living Vision experiment has unfolded, many people have asked me to clarify our relationship to the Church. This is a difficult question for me. In fairness to the communities that hosted and welcomed me so graciously throughout this book project, I must acknowledge that they all see themselves and their communities as *part of* the Church with a capital C. Each leader who participated in this project was very clear about his/her deep commitment to the Church, as it presently exists.

None of them see themselves as presenting some sort of alternative to the larger institutional Church, and they wanted to be sure that I not portray them as such. I hope I have honored their wishes.

But unlike the communities I visited, I tend to think of where we are in Christian history as a "post-Church" age. To me, the institutional Church is on an irreversible decline, and thus I've chosen to concern myself with how followers of Jesus might configure ourselves and live out our discipleship when the Church is no longer an option, either because of its irrelevance or its extinction.

Admittedly, with so much of my experience in the institutional Church feeling so far away from the pathway of Jesus, I am open about my search for some sort of alternative for the growing millions who simply can't see Jesus in the gatherings and practices of what we've come to call "church." In fact, a big part of me has come to wonder whether the very word "church" might be too laden with baggage and corruption to ever be linked to the Way of Jesus again. This is why terms like Brian McLaren's "community of practice" are so appealing to me, as I try to move myself and others further along the path of Christ.

In the final analysis, I suppose I don't care much whether it is within the church or outside it that we find our way to the Way of Jesus. What I do care deeply about is that we get there and that we illuminate that path—the path of Jesus—in an authentic, meaningful, and humble way. If this little book and our Living Vision community can be a part of lighting that path, then my life and work will have been worth the effort.

In the evolution of the structure of this book and the research that solidified it, I restricted my observations about each community to that particular chapter's focus. I'd like to dedicate these final pages to making a few general observations about practices and characteristics these amazing and gracious communities share in common.

1. OPEN THEOLOGY

All the communities I visited were open to a broad range of beliefs, and none had any theological litmus tests to bar anyone from connecting with their community. I think the language of Nanette Sawyer at Wicker Park Grace accurately represents all the communities I visited when she said, "There is a center toward which we are moving, but no borders or boundaries that separate us from others."[1] The sense in all these communities was that theology, even at its best, is and always has been constructed by humans trying to express the inexpressible, and, therefore, we should all join in that on-going, never ending endeavor with the appropriate humility and energy. In all of my visits, no one was ever afraid to express doubts, questions, or even objections to particular Christian doctrines or beliefs. It is the dialogue and discussion that matter most in these relationally driven communities, not uniformity or agreement. This process orientation may explain why all of these communities warmly included people who had never made any sort of confession of faith.

2. NO MEMBERSHIP

Each and every community I studied was intentional about avoiding the notion of membership.[2]* The idea of members and non-members struck them as more appropriate for a country club or fraternity than for a group of Christ followers. Anyone who wanted to involve him/herself with these communities at any level and to any extent was welcome to do so. I did notice that several of the alternative communities struggled to find or even create the best language for those regular participants in their shared life and work, but any terms that carried a sense of an in-group and an out-group were rejected. The most common word I heard was "participant," and that was used without any sense of the extent or duration of one's involvement. If one attended and participated in any aspect of the community's life, no matter how often, he/she was a welcome "participant."

3. ARTS FOCUSED

The walls of each congregation's meeting place, whether owned or rented, were filled with paintings, drawings, photography, and other original works of art. Most often the artists who produced these works were participants in that particular spiritual community, although in some cases the community was simply recognizing and celebrating the work of a

1. Sawyer, interview.

2. This aversion to the idea of membership was not as true of The Simple Way and Camden Community House. People interested in their communities must progress through a series of steps modeled after the monastic orders of old. Candidates begin with the novitiate phase and gradually develop spiritual disciplines and practices that are necessary for life in their communities.

local artist who was not involved in their community. This orientation toward celebrating artistic expression seemed to grow out of a theology that recognized God as the Creator, the Artist who endowed us with the ability and desire to express ourselves as well. It was truly inspiring to walk through each community's facility and see such living, contemporary expressions of art everywhere I looked. This reverence for and participation in artistic expression went well beyond the visual arts; it was reflected in the music of each community as well. Most of the communities I visited had participants who wrote music for the community's gatherings and liturgies. Those who didn't compose used their creativity to put together amazingly original arrangements of existing songs that reflected the overall vibe of the community. As a professional performing musician myself, I was both impressed and moved by all the music I experienced in these exemplary communities. I am also keenly aware of the huge amount of time and labor their volunteer musicians must have put forth in order to bring such creations into being.

It is also important to note that just because some of these resurrection communities write so much of their own liturgical material, one should not assume that they are without ritual. Ritual and recurring practices play a significant role in all of the communities I visited; it's just that some of the material they use ritualistically is more contemporary or even still in process. Several of the groups I included in my research regularly used ancient practices and liturgies very effectively, even with young worshippers. Mindless, inherited ritual can be deadening to those seeking spiritual truth. But thoughtful, understood, recurring practices can both ground and deepen one's experience of the divine. It is this second type of ritual that I encountered in my sojourning.

4. FLAT STRUCTURE/EMPOWERING LEADERSHIP

The pastors of these communities were rarely, if ever, the center of attention, even and particularly in the worship gatherings. A broad range of people participated in, planned, executed, and even led many of the significant events and ministries in the lives of these congregations. The participants clearly "owned" and took responsibility for whatever the congregation was up to. None of the resurrection communities I visited had committees or complicated processes to bring ideas to fruition. Whatever programs existed had clearly bubbled up from the congregation; they didn't trickle down from the top. Participants were very bright, very assertive, and saw themselves on equal footing with their pastors. The pastors were without egos and reveled in their congregation's energy, creativity, and initiative. This was perhaps most noticeable in the "sermon" portion of each community's worship gatherings. Even in this high moment of any pastor's life, these innovative, empowering leaders chose to include their communities in both the planning and execution of the sermon and the entire service as well. In many cases, the pastors converted their sermons—traditionally thought of as monologues—into lively, multi-voice conversations, literally inviting comments throughout the enterprise. The pastor as facilitator model was much more prevalent in these resurrection communities than was the pastor as expert model.

5. CHANGE WAS CONSTANT AND EMBRACED

The congregations and communities I studied had been through constant and substantial changes without splitting apart. The language participants used to talk about their spiritual home was in the present progressive tense, including phrases like "what we're doing now is," and "we recently started," and "we'll see how this goes and then re-evaluate." Change was neither feared nor resisted in these resurrection communities. It was embraced as a fact of life, one that was apt to bring positive opportunities and Christlike spontaneity to the community. There was a pervasive attitude among these post-church communities that even when an attempt at change didn't work out, there was no cause for regret or second-guessing. Experimentation is a regular facet of their existence and so are any results of such experiments. Moving onto the next attempt at following Christ seemed far more important than lamenting the previous one.

6. YOUNGER FOLKS WERE THE NORM

While age was by no means frowned upon in any of these communities, the vast majority of people in the communities I visited were between twenty and forty-five. The upside of such a youthful composition is a tremendous sense of openness, vitality, energy, and creativity. The downside is that people in their twenties and thirties tend to move around a lot for things like graduate school or new job opportunities. These communities, therefore, have to get used to saying goodbye to and then replacing key leaders and participants on a regular basis. Younger participants also tend to have less disposable income to devote to communal causes and projects than do later career folks and retirees. Another detriment for any spiritual community that lacks middle aged and elderly participants is a lack of wisdom, experience, and perspective. Being in community with brothers and sisters who are approaching death or have lost a long-time partner is also extremely valuable where spiritual depth and authenticity are desired.

7. WORSHIP GATHERINGS ARE CASUAL AND RELAXED

People in the communities where I sojourned did not dress up for worship or any other church gatherings. Even in worship, participants drifted casually in and out of the room without interrupting anything. Often coffee or tea was brought into the worship space or even served there, and no one balked at occasional texting or twittering during the service. Participants were free to speak up, whether in the form of an "Amen," a humorous remark, or even a question asked out loud. There was a tacit understanding that all of worship—including the sermon—is a dialogue in which all participate equally.

8. FOCUSED IN MISSION & SERVICE

These congregations and communities do a lot of significant, deep, relational service, but in a very narrow and targeted way. Each community tended to have only one or two outreach projects rather than a bunch of little, hit and run efforts aimed at various groups of people. They do a lot of wholistic work with and for a particular community, so that their partnership and impact run deep instead of broad. Most often, the particular Christian community had created a 501(c)(3) and then developed several significant partnerships with non-Christian organizations and NGO's, so that together they could help the people they were serving to experience more immediate, effective, lasting, and comprehensive change.

9. INTEGRATION & WHOLENESS

Rob Bell's notion of everything being spiritual is very much at play in these communities. The distinction between sacred and secular has been eradicated in resurrection communities. Being a person of faith in these communities means that what you eat and what you buy, where you live and what you spend your money on, the kind of car you drive, and the environmental footprint you are leaving are every bit as important to God as reading the Bible or attending worship gatherings. Most of these communities not only meet in very artsy places but offer and encourage things like yoga and community gardening.

I like the way Tony Jones talks about spiritual integrity in his book *The New Christians:*

> Most human activity is inherently theological, in that it reflects what we believe to be the case about God . . . The house I buy—where it is, how big it is, how much it costs—*is* a theological decision. It reflects what I believe about the following questions and more: Does God care where I live? Does God care how I spend my money? Does God care about energy use? Does God favor public transportation? Maybe I believe that God cares about none of these things, in which case my decision to purchase the biggest house I can afford in the nicest part of town reflects my theological belief that God is not concerned with such things . . . So theology isn't just talk . . . Virtually everything we do is inherently theological. Almost every choice we make reflects what we think about God. There's no escaping it.[3]

This is the thinking I found in each of the communities I visited. If one's faith doesn't have an impact on the car he buys, the food he consumes, and the waste he generates, what good is it?

10. PRACTICE OF SPIRITUAL DISCIPLINES

Most of the resurrection communities I studied not only appreciate but actually teach and practice ancient spiritual disciplines. As Shane Claiborne of The Simple Way put it, "the word 'disciple' comes from the word 'discipline.'"[4] So it shouldn't surprise us that these resurrection communities practice things like prayer, fasting, the daily office, lectio divina, the year of jubilee, incomplete harvesting, and others. There is also deep regard, even in the newest of the communities I visited, for those who have gone before us in the faith, particularly the Monastics. Many of the communities I visited are part of the "New Monasticism" movement, where the actual practice of and living of spiritual disciplines is seen as essential for discipleship or apprenticeship to Jesus.

3. Tony Jones, *The New Christians*, 106.
4. Shane Claiborne, interview.

~

In closing, it is important to note that despite the common threads and principles shared by the communities featured in this work, each one was distinct in its embodiment of Jesus' way. These are not communities that are shopping around to import the latest and greatest practices from elsewhere, but rather each has done the hard work of determining what Christ's path looks like for them in their particular context. In that light, it is not my intention that Christian communities who read this book will treat it like a spiritual smorgasbord, picking a practice here and a program there to plug in at their home church. I hope I have made it clear that the kind of change I am advocating and the kind of change Christ needs from those bearing his name is complete, core level change, major paradigmatic repentance.

I would be grateful if those who have taken the time to read this book would email me and share your journeys and experiences along the Way of Jesus. I have much to learn from you and would welcome your insights. Grace and peace to all my fellow travelers on the Way of Jesus.

Bibliography

Archives of the Glide Memorial United Methodist Church, Social Action/Social Justice, San Francisco, CA.

Bassett, Kate. 2008. Interview by author. Tape recording. Harbor Springs, MI., 14 December.

Bullhorn: Nooma Video Series, 009. Produced and directed by Flannel. 12 minutes. Zondervan, 2005. Digital Video Disc.

Bell, Rob. *Velvet Elvis: Repainting The Christian Faith.* Grand Rapids: Zondervan, 2005.

Bolt, John A. "No Pastor? No Problem." *Presbyterians Today* 99 (2009.)

Brown Taylor, Barbara. *An Altar in the World: A Geography of Faith.* New York: Harper One, 2009.

Buchanan, John. "Something Christlike," *Christian Century.* July 29, 2008.

Buechner, Frederick. *Listening to Your Life.* New York: Harper One, 1992.

Carl III, William J. ed, *Best Advice: Wisdom on Ministry from 30 Leading Pastors and Preachers.* Louisville: Westminster John Knox Press, 2009.

Carl III, William J. "Preaching in a Church Where the Culture Needs to Change." In *Best Advice,* edited by William J. Carl III, (Louisville: Westminster John Knox Press, 2009), 40.

Carson, D. A. *Becoming Conversant With The Emerging Church.* Grand Rapids: Zondervan, 2005

Claiborne, Shane. *The Irresistible Revolution.* Grand Rapids: Zondervan, 2006.

Claiborne, Shane. 2009. Telephone conversation with the author, 21 July.

Davies, Denny et al. *Jansen's History of Art: The Western Tradition.* Upper Saddle River: Pearson/Prentice Hall.

Deboni, Jake, and Jess Rozga. 2009. Interview by author. Tape recording. Noodles Restaurant, Chicago, 21 April.

Dickelman, Tom. 2009. Interview by author. Tape recording. Union Station, Chicago, 21 April.

Frampton, Don. 2008. Interview by author. St. Charles Avenue Presbyterian Church, New Orleans, 29 Oct.

———. 2008. Sermon preached at First Presbyterian Church, 10 August, Harbor Springs, MI.

Friedman, Thomas. *The World is Flat, A Brief History of the Twenty-first Century.* New York: Picador, 2005.

Fry, Sister Rose Marie. 2009. Interview by author. Tape recording. The Sisters of St. Joseph compound, Cap Haitien, Haiti, 21 January.

Green, Amy. "Finding My Religion." *Sojourners* (2008) June.

Grenz, Stanley. *Created for Community.* Grand Rapids: Baker Books, 1998.

Haw, Chris. 2009. Telephone conversation with the author, 16 August.

Heath, Elaine. 2009. Telephone conversation with the author, 28 July.

———. *The Mystic Way of Evangelism*. Grand Rapids: Baker Books, 2008.

Hillestad, Luke. 2009. Interview by author. Solomon's Porch art studio, 5 May.

Hillestad, Michelle. 2009. Interview by author. Solomon's Porch art studio, 5 May.

Howell, James C. "Don't Take My Advice." In *Best Advice: Wisdom on Ministry from 30 Leading Pastors and Preachers,* edited by William J. Carl III, (Louisville: Westminster John Knox Press, 2009), 40.

Johnson, Ben. 2009. Telephone conversation with the author, 4 May.

Jones, Tony. *The New Christians: Dispatches from the Emergent Frontier.* San Francisco: Jossey-Bass, 2008.

Jones, Tony, and Doug Pagitt. *An Emergent Manifesto of Hope.* Grand Rapids: Baker Books, 2007.

J. R. 2009. Interview by author front. Tape recording. The Church of the Holy Apostles, New York, 12 May.

Kinnaman, David, and Gabe Lyons. *unchristian,* Grand Rapids: Baker Books, 2007.

Kirk-Davidoff, Heather. "Meeting Jesus at the Bar." In *An Emergent Manifesto of Hope*, edited by Doug Pagitt and Tony Jones, (Grand Rapids: Baker Books, 2007), 35.

Maxwell, Liz. 2009. Interview by author. Tape recording. Her office in Church of the Holy Apostles, New York, 12 May.

McBride, Dustin. "Enjoying the 'In-Between' Times." *Sojourners,* June, (2008).

Murchi, Kristi. 2009. Interview by author. The sanctuary of Solomon's Porch, 3 May.

McLaren, Brian D. *Finding Our Way Again, The Return of the Ancient Practices.* Nashville: Thomas Nelson, 2008

Pagitt, Doug. *Reimagining Spiritual Formation: A Week in the Life of an Experimental Church.* Grand Rapids: Zondervan, 2003.

———. *A Christianity Worth Believing: Hope-Filled, Open-Armed, Alive-And-WellFaith For The Left Out, Left Behind, And Let Down In Us All.* San Francisco: Jossey-Bass, 2008.

———. 2009. Interview by author. Tape recording. Minneapolis coffee shop, 4 May.

Reed, Janean Silvia. 2009. Interview by author. Tape recording. Glide Memorial United Methodist Church, 28 April.

Richmond, David. 2009. Interview by author. Tape recording. Glide Memorial United Methodist Church, 27 April.

Sawyer, Nanette. 2009. Interview by author. Tape recording. Wicker Park coffee shop, Chicago, 20 April.

———. *Hospitality—the sacred art: Discovering the Hidden Spiritual Power of Invitation and Welcome.* Woodstock: Skylight Paths, 2008.

Spong, John Shelby. *The Sins of Scripture: Exposing the Bible's Texts of Hate to Reveal the God of Love.* San Francisco: Harper Collins, 2005.

St. Francis Parish, Scituate, Mass. 2009. Interview by Anne Thompson. *The Today Show.* National Broadcasting Company, 12 May.

Tickle, Phyllis. *The Great Emergence: How Christianity is Changing and Why.* Grand Rapids: Baker Books, 2008.

Viola, Frank. *Reimagining Church.* Colorado Springs: David C. Cook, 2008.

Viola, Frank, and George Barna, *Pagan Christianity*. Carol Stream: Barna Books/Tyndale House, 2007.

Walter, Mark. 2009. Interview by author. Tape recording. The Church of the Holy Apostles kitchen, 12 May.

Willard, Dallas. *The Divine Conspiracy: Rediscovering Our Hidden Life In God.* New York: Harper One, 1997.

Williams, Cecil B. *I Am Alive.* New York: Harper and Row, 1980.

Williams, Cecil B., and Janice Mirikitani. 2009. Interview by author. Tape recording. Glide Memorial United Methodist Church, 29 April.

Wilson-Hartgrove, Jonathan. *The New Monasticism: What It Has To Say To Today's Church.* Grand Rapids: Brazos Press, 2008.

X, Bob. 2009. Interview by author. Tape recording. The Church of the Holy Apostles sanctuary, 12 May.

X, Gene. 2009. Interview by author. Tape recording. The Church of the Holy Apostles sanctuary, 12 May.